ROLE PLAYING

The Instructional Design Library
Volume 32

ROLE PLAYING

Wallace Wohlking
Cornell University
New York

and

Patricia J. Gill
Bernard Hodes Advertising, Inc.
New York

Danny G. Langdon
Series Editor

Educational Technology Publications
Englewood Cliffs, New Jersey 07632

Library of Congress Cataloging in Publication Data

Wohlking, Wallace.
    Role playing.

    (The Instructional design library; v. 32)
    Bibliography: p.
    1. Role playing. I. Gill, Patricia J., joint
author. II. Title. III. Series: Instructional
design library; v. 32.
LB1069.W63   371.3   79-23435
ISBN 0-87778-152-4

Printed in the United States of America.

Library of Congress Catalog Card Number:
79-23435.

International Standard Book Number:
0-87778-152-4.

First Printing: March, 1980.

FOREWORD

I have always been fascinated by role plays. Perhaps it is the bit of actor or actress in each of us. One thing that always troubled me, however, was the purpose that playing out a role was to achieve, other than the obvious one of experiencing a problem situation. I am happy to report that Wallace Wohlking and Patricia J. Gill clearly tell us what can be achieved from effective role plays.

Most of us who have participated in role plays or, I suspect, designed them for others, have probably been used to only one format. This format involves two or three students getting up and acting out a scenario of parts that have been given to them. Usually, this is an open-ended scenario without structure—or at least we don't perceive a structure. As the authors so clearly point out, there are actually two overall approaches, and within each, three possible structures. This, it seems to me, opens up the possibility of many kinds of role plays for various environments and needs. Role play is not just one strategy. Whether you look upon role play as two overall strategies or six specific ones, we would do well to carefully select that which best fits each learning situation. Ample illustrations of all are in this book.

Danny G. Langdon
Series Editor

PREFACE

Role playing is used in many different ways. It has been used by sociologists to determine factors affecting motivation and attitude change. It is used in a form known as psychodrama by clinical psychologists for psychiatric diagnoses. There is a long history of its use for assessments of qualities thought to be useful in certain tasks and positions. The first use in this form started with the German army in the 1930's as a screening device in the selection of army recruits. Role playing as a tool designed to predict success in specified job functions is now coming into widespread use in the assessment centers which have been created by many of America's leading corporations.

The major use of role playing, however, is in the area of training and education. Though a variety of books and articles have been written about the use of role playing in training, at the time of this writing, no one book exists which takes the trainer through the entire role-playing process, complete with detailed instructions on how to deal with each step. This book has been written to fill that vacuum.

We would like to thank Carol Wittenberg, Daryl Wohlking, Sheila Barnes, Georgette Deroche, and Rochelle Semel for their thoughtful reading of various portions of the manuscript. Their comments and reactions were helpful in formulating ideas and concepts presented in this book. We appreciate Malcolm Shaw for his contributions related to the sections, "An Initial Sales Presentation" and "Giving Feedback." We would also like to thank Marge Baxter for her editorial assistance and Dick Fenton for typing the major part of the manuscript. Lastly, our thanks to the Extension Division of the New York State School of Industrial and Labor Relations, Cornell University, for providing the logistical support that permitted and facilitated the preparation of the manuscript.

W.W.
P.J.G.

CONTENTS

ABSTRACT

ROLE PLAYING

Role Playing specifically focuses on the training dimensions of this subject. It identifies the sequence necessary to conduct role-playing sessions: (1) determination of training objectives; and (2) outlining of the three phases of role playing: (a) the warm-up, (b) the enactment, and (c) the post-enactment discussion. In addition, it distinguishes between the use of method-centered and developmental role playing and gives guidelines for the appropriate use of each type. The book includes information on how to: (1) create steps related to method-centered role plays; (2) write roles for role-playing cases; and (3) develop and use observer guides for use during role-playing enactments.

ROLE PLAYING

I.

USE

"Suit the action to the word, the word to the action."—Hamlet

Introduction

We live in a world that has seen an increasing use of education to achieve good jobs and to enhance personal effectiveness on the job. Our society uses formal education to train its members for work paths in the professional, business, and industrial world. However, one of the well-known facts about education is that it does not necessarily guarantee effective job performance.

One of the most common causes of failure in work performance has to do with ineffectiveness in dealing with people face-to-face. Illustrations of this abound in all fields. Typical examples are the person who learns the principles of selling, but can't sell; the union steward who knows the collective bargaining agreement better than the personnel manager but loses the grievance; and the technically brilliant manager who alienates subordinates in attempts to communicate. To extend the list, there are the well-trained and able doctor and nurse who are unable to project that expertise, and the teacher and lawyer who have the facts but cannot help others to use those facts. Essentially, the breakdown comes when one-to-one communication, so essential to work success, is ineffective. That breakdown can be with superiors, subordinates, clients, patients, students, or peers.

3

Obviously, many people are unable to translate their understanding of communications into effective behavior. The objective of this book is to describe how the role-playing technique can be used by trainers and teachers to assist participants to handle more effectively a large number of interpersonal problems that occur in business and social situations. This book shows how the process of role playing, an educational or therapeutic technique in which a life situation, typically involving conflict, is developed and acted out. The enactment is then followed by a discussion or analysis to determine what happened, to whom, how the problem/conflict was resolved, and possibly how the problem/conflict might be better resolved in the future.

Not only can role playing help people close the gap between what they know and how they apply it, but also it can serve as a training method to deal with almost any type of situation where face-to-face transactions are involved. For this purpose, it is used by such diverse organizations as business corporations, public schools, police training academies, and psychiatric hospitals to teach personnel in all levels of the organization, from president to clerk, principal to guidance counselor, physician to orderly, to perform their jobs more effectively.

Table 1 indicates some of the major uses of role playing in training situations. It can be seen that role playing, after sensitivity training, is the preferred training method of training directors (as reflected in a national survey) to develop interpersonal skills or to change attitudes. It should be pointed out that because of the high cost and extensive time demands of sensitivity training, for many trainers it is often not a *practical* training option. Thus, in effect, this makes role playing the first practical choice for most trainers who have a responsibility for developing interpersonal skills or changing attitudes.

Table 1

Effectiveness of Selected Training Methods
for Achieving Training Objectives
(Based on a national sample of training directors*)

Training Methods	Training Objectives					
	Interpersonal Skills	Changing Attitudes	Problem-Solving Skills	Knowledge Retention	Participant Acceptance	Knowledge Acquisition
	Mean Rank	Mean Rank	Mean Rank	Mean Rank	Mean Rank	Mean Rank
Sensitivity Training	1	1	5	3	6	8
Role Playing	2	2	3	4	4	7
Conference (Discussion) Method	3	3	4	5	1	3
Lecture (with questions)	8	8	9	8	8	9
Business Games	5	5	2	6	3	6
Movie Films	6	6	7	7	5	4
Case Study	4	4	1	2	2	2
Television Lecture	9	9	8	9	9	5
Programmed Instruction	7	7	6	1	7	1

*All data on training objectives at .01 level of significance.

Based on: Nash, A.N., J.P. Muczyk, and F.L. Vettori. The Relative Practical Effectiveness of Programmed Instruction. *Personnel Psychology*, 1971, 397-418, Table 1.

Two Basic Forms of Role Playing

There are two major forms of role playing: (1) method-centered role playing, and (2) developmental role playing. Method-centered role playing is used primarily to develop skills in specific procedures, methods, and techniques. It is a form of role playing that tends to deal with frequently recurring situations which lend themselves to being treated on a procedural basis. Typically, these situations and problems are of relatively short duration. Developmental role playing is used to deal with relatively complex situations for which it is not normally possible to develop a set of step-by-step procedures. The two major uses of developmental role playing involve (1) training people in attitudinal areas (learning about attitudes and motivations—oneself as well as others), and (2) integrating and applying learning from a variety of sources to deal with problem situations.

The primary differences between the two methods are that (1) method-centered role playing provides a specific structure and/or approach to deal with a problem situation, whereas developmental role playing does not. (2) In method-centered role playing, less emphasis is placed on issues related to feelings and attitudes, whereas in developmental role playing, discussion of attitudes will often be the key ingredient of the role-playing experience.

Method-Centered Role Playing

A wide variety of procedures is taught through method-centered role playing. The common denominator of this training method is that the trainee is provided with a defined and structured approach when responding to specified situations. That is, the trainee is given a series of steps or guidelines to follow in order to handle the procedure. Situations that would fall into this category would be those that tend to be simple and recurring, such as:

- registering a new student;

- taking an incoming office call;
- admitting a new patient;
- making a routine banking transaction; or
- dealing with a customer returning merchandise.

The objective of this training is to provide trainees with reliable and consistent techniques to handle these types of transactions. Two occupational groups which are required to perform many short-term transactions are salespersons and supervisors, the very two groups which receive the greatest amount of method-centered role playing. Other groups engaging in transactions of relatively short duration—bank clerks, receptionists, flight attendants—also receive a large amount of method-centered role-playing training.

Developmental Role Playing

Developmental role playing is characterized by a situation in which the trainee is confronted with a problem. In this problem situation, the trainee must spontaneously deal with whatever issue is at hand. No specific steps or guidelines are given to respond to the situation. This technique may be used to explore the feelings and attitudes that are engendered by such problem situations so that the trainee can better understand his or her own motivation as well as that of others. This understanding normally enhances the trainee's ability to be more effective in handling interpersonal transactions.

Developmental role playing is also used to develop skills in a large number of areas which do not easily lend themselves to being proceduralized or taught in a step-by-step fashion. Subjects commonly taught include:

- Communication Skills
- Non-directive Interviewing
- Counseling
- Problem-Solving
- Contract Negotiations
- Arbitration
- Conference Leadership
- Joint Goal Setting

Developmental role playing, as contrasted to method-centered role playing, allows the trainee to experiment with different approaches and solutions when confronted with a problem. By trying out these possibilities, the trainee may judge for himself or herself which approach might be the most successful in any given situation. Participants can fail and not suffer the consequences, then go on to practice another approach. They are allowed an opportunity to integrate and apply previous learnings in action situations and judge their success. This form of role playing also allows the trainee to determine how appropriate his or her attitudes and motivations are when responding to a particular problem.

Other Uses of Role Playing

Developmental role playing, in addition to being a training tool in its own right, can often be used as a supplemental tool in conjunction with other methods, e.g., to try out the possibility of certain solutions arrived at in case study exercises. In problem-solving meetings, specific courses of action can be experimented with through role playing. It is also a technique used within the context of sensitivity training groups or T-groups to demonstrate and analyze group phenomena related to status issues, polarization, hidden agenda items, and concern with tools over process issues.

Role playing of *all* types is most commonly used as a group exercise. An integral part of the process requires group feedback to the role players concerning reactions to role-play enactments. In role playing, a mutual learning takes place in that the role players are dependent on the group to learn how their actions will be perceived and understood. Also, the group learns from the role players the types of behaviors which appear to be effective as well as those actions which are counterproductive.

Role playing is more rarely used as a kind of tutorial exercise. In this case, one person (a consultant, teacher, counselor, lawyer, etc.) may perform both the role of teacher and that of a participating role player. The "teacher," in effect, will aid those who would like to increase their skills in handling a particular problem or interpersonal conflict.

The "teacher" places the client into a problem setting and plays the other role himself or herself. For example, the problem might be that of the subordinate who is creating a difficulty. The client then tries out an approach on the "teacher." At the completion of the role play, the "teacher" gives his or her reaction regarding the client's effectiveness. This one-to-one approach is most often used when one person would like assistance regarding a special problem that requires immediate attention and/or confidentiality.

The role-playing technique can be used with almost any age group, from elementary children on up. The designs explained in this book can be applied to any job setting. However, the illustrations will be primarily related to work settings where role playing today already has extensive use.

To the extent that the subject material is highly technical and subject-matter centered, role playing is not an appropriate teaching method, whereas such subjects as conflict resolution, psychology, counseling, and managing people offer numerous opportunities for use of the method. However, even within the areas in which role playing is appropriate, its content should never be overly complex. Role playing requires that people interact with other people in a defined context, and exercise in this area should never be burdened with technical complexities that may serve to cloud the *human* dimension of the exercise.

Role playing, then, is used to broaden people's repertoire of behaviors and to help them gain insight into their present behavior and possibly to modify it. Role playing gives people an opportunity to try out behavior before mistakes are made in a real-life situation.

II.

OPERATIONAL DESCRIPTION

Introduction

This chapter is an introduction and overview of how role-playing sessions can be planned and conducted. There will be a discussion of how to (1) relate training objectives to the choice of a training method, (2) decide on method-centered role playing or developmental role playing, (3) decide on one of three types of role playing, and (4) conduct the three phases of the role-playing sessions: the warm-up, the enactment, and the post-enactment discussion. A chart at the end of this chapter visually depicts this process. In addition, there will be a discussion of the educational assumptions underlying both method-centered and developmental role playing.

Training Objectives

No discussion of role playing can be meaningful which does not relate the training method to the trainer's objectives. The trainer must first diagnose the problem he or she is trying to remedy and then decide on a course of action.

Assuming, for example, that two key objectives in any supervisory training problem would be (1) the improvement of interpersonal skills and (2) the development of appropriate attitudes for dealing with employees, the trainer would want to choose a training method that was effective in achieving these goals.

Two Educational Approaches to Role Playing

To increase the effectiveness of training in achieving given educational goals and targets, it is necessary first to examine certain underlying dimensions of the educational process: (1) didactic vs. discovery-oriented education; (2) method-centered role playing as a didactic approach to skill development; and (3) developmental role playing as a discovery-oriented approach to skill development and behavior change.

The two basic approaches to the educational process will be designated as the didactic and the discovery-oriented approach.

Didactic Education

Didactic education is characterized by (1) a sequential presentation of data; (2) input originated from a teacher, film, machine, or printed pages; and (3) the use of external motivation. In general, didactic education aims for predictable results, such as raising the reading level of a person or a class from X level to Y level in a specified period of time.

A typical example of a didactic educational approach is the lecture. Here the student listens, may take notes, and generally attempts to relate such input to his or her existing body of knowledge. An efficient and updated method of didactic education is programmed learning. Here the trainee learns sequentially, from limited and defined input. It deviates from pure didactic education in that the rate of speed governing student learning is self-controlled.

Discovery-Oriented Learning

In contrast, discovery-oriented learning is characterized by (1) a relative lack of structure and sequence; (2) the random development of insights by the trainee as he or she experiences, interprets, and reacts to certain stimuli; and (3) an important degree of control over the pace of the learning process by the student. Also, discovery-oriented education often stresses learning from other students and peers who are present during the learning experience. In general, it encourages learning by exposing the student to challenging educational stimuli and removing the pressures characteristic of sequential teaching.

In discovery-oriented learning, the amount and quality of the learning is much less predictable than with didactic learning.

Method-Centered Role Playing

Method-centered role playing is based primarily on a didactic approach to achieving an educational objective. The trainee is given a clear-cut set of guidelines to solve a problem or deal with a situation. When confronted with a problem in the context of a role play, he or she applies the guidelines (method) to deal with it. Typically, if the student has conscientiously followed the method, the problem will be dealt with or handled appropriately. If the trainee uses the same method several times when responding to a problem, he or she will tend to develop confidence dealing with similar situations in real life.

Many of the training objectives relate to handling routine and recurring situations. In these cases, the choice of method-centered role playing is indicated, particularly if a procedure or sequence has been developed for handling these problems. The general nature of the problem is known to the person performing the role; i.e., the briefing will specify that the problem has to do with handling an employee complaint, and the role player is given a set of guidelines or steps for handling the problem.

Developmental Role Playing

Developmental role playing represents an example of the discovery-oriented approach to education. In this role play, a student must improvise and react spontaneously to the situation. During the role play, it is unclear just what is being learned. The learning which seems to be taking place appears to be without sequence and not just subject to any standard educational criteria.

A common characteristic of most well-conducted developmental role plays (as in well-designed discovery learning situations) is the "ah-ha" experience. Typically, this happens when a student, attempting to adapt to an ambiguous situation (a characteristic of most discovery learning stimuli), suddenly sees the relationship of two ideas; or in a role play, the trainee suddenly realizes the impact of his or her behavior on another person and becomes more aware of the dynamics of the situation.

In dealing with an interpersonal problem in a role play, the trainee may begin to alter his or her usual method of handling certain situations. This modification of behavior often results in more effective interactions. As a result of several small role-play success experiences of this type, he or she may start to revise his or her approach to similar situations in real life.

In developmental role playing, the trainee is confronted by a situation in which only a symptom of a problem is known. For example, the briefing sheet for the role player might say that "your subordinate has been acting sullen recently and you would like to find out why." Or, the role play may be so complex that no set of steps can be given in advance that will prove useful in solving the role-playing problem. The developmental role typically demands of the trainee that he or she integrate and apply previously acquired learning in dealing with the role player's problem.

Common Denominator of Role Playing

The primary objective of most role-playing efforts is to develop skills, and/or modify, change, influence, or teach new behavior. In some cases, the effort to achieve behavior change is focused on learning a simple procedure, e.g., how to answer a telephone. Other efforts may be focused on providing the student with insight into his or her own motivations and behavior. Whether the training objectives are focused on achieving a modest or a deep change in behavior, the common denominator of all role playing is *learning through experience.*

To summarize, the trainer must (1) identify training objectives; (2) choose a method or a combination of training methods which will achieve the objectives; and (3) decide whether the training problem (assuming role playing is the method chosen) should utilize method-centered role play or a developmental role play.

Three Types of Role Playing

There are three major forms of role playing: (1) single role plays; (2) role rotational role plays; and (3) multiple role plays.

Single Role Plays

Single role plays are indicated when the group is small (eight to 12) (thereby reducing possible trainee anxiety) and/or when it is possible that all or most will have an opportunity to go through a similar experience in the session. This method is helpful, as is the case with role rotational role play, when the trainer wants to give the group a shared experience which can stimulate discussion and analysis based on observations of the trainees watching the role play.

Role Rotational Role Plays

Role rotational role plays require different trainees to role play the same problem with one person who remains constant. Example: A salesperson is required to sell something to a customer. Someone in the group takes the role of customer. Then two, three, or four other trainees, in sequence, play the salesperson and attempt to sell the customer. This method is often used to demonstrate how different people using approximately the same method will employ varied styles.

Multiple Role Plays

Multiple role plays involve the entire class and require that the trainees simultaneously assume roles in a given case. For example, if the class is working on the case of a supervisor dealing with a poorly motivated employee, divide the class into groups of three. In each group will be a supervisor, an employee, and an observer. All groups will simultaneously role play the same case.

Three Functional Phases of Role Playing

A role playing session consists of three phases: (1) the warm-up, (2) the enactment, and (3) the post-enactment discussion. Each has an important and basic purpose.

The Warm-Up

The warm-up is designed to motivate trainee participation in the role play. All warm-ups are focused to some degree on a problem which confronts the trainee or will confront him or her. Particularly in developmental role plays, it is necessary to: (1) develop interest, and, if possible, enthusiasm about the focus of the role-playing activity; and (2) reduce trainee anxiety about entering into a role-playing situation. Whether or not the trainer uses a method-centered or a developmental role play, the warm-up is used for all role-play training experiences.

The Enactment

The key elements in conducting the enactment involve (1) selecting the players, (2) setting the scene of the role play, (3) starting the action, and (4) intervening when appropriate.

Selecting Role Players: After the warm-up, the trainer is ready to start the action. The trainer will need trainees to participate in the role play. He or she can select role players or ask for volunteers. After the role players have been identified, the trainer will then instruct them on their roles. Normally, he or she will have briefing sheets (short statements which describe to the participants the roles they are to take). (Illustrative briefing sheets are provided in the Appendix to this book.) Or, the trainer may simply brief the role players orally, instructing them on their roles in front of the group. Example: "You have just been informed that a friend of yours is unhappy working with you and has asked for a transfer from the department. You want to talk to him about it."

Setting the Scene: The trainer must now create the setting for the role play. This he or she does by having the group read the general information sheet about the situation to be role played. Or, the trainer can do this orally. An example of an oral briefing would be: "The PTA has had a big drop in its membership meetings in recent months. This seems to be related to faculty-parent friction. The president of the PTA is now about to meet with the head of the teachers' group." The trainer also briefly describes the physical setting of the scene. Example: "The scene you are about to see takes place in John's office. John is sitting here (trainer points to a chair) and Lee is standing there."

Starting the Action: Typically, the trainer will instruct the role players to start the action. The trainer may also facilitate the start of action with a comment on how the action starts. Example: "As the scene opens, John has just entered the room. He starts by greeting Lee."

Interventions: Normally, there are no interventions in the course of method-centered role playing. However, in developmental role playing, intervention is frequently used. Interventions are desirable when one of the trainees is having serious trouble in handling the role assigned, or when the trainer wants the role players to gain insight into another person's situation or feelings. This can be done through the process of role reversal, which is discussed in detail in the next chapter. Normally, all role plays should be allowed to continue to completion of the interaction. However, when the role players start to become repetitive, or when the key points which the trainer wanted to surface during the role plays are made, he or she should intervene and bring the role play to a close.

The Post-Enactment Discussion

The basic purpose of the discussion following the role-playing activity is to assist in crystallizing the experience in such a way that the role players and the observing group can better understand whatever took place during the enactment. This is best facilitated by clearly separating content and process issues and discussing and giving feedback on each. The class shares their reactions to the enactment, the role players themselves react to their experience, and the trainer may provide feedback.

The nature of the feedback, to an important extent, is determined by whether the role play was method-centered or developmental. In method-centered role playing, the discussion tends to focus specifically on the extent to which the role players followed the guidelines which were presented in the warm-up.

To a lesser extent, the trainer focuses on the attitudes which surfaced during the role play. In other words, a prime emphasis in a post-enactment discussion of a method-centered role play is to reinforce behavior which related to the use of a specific set of guidelines or a procedure.

In a developmental role play, emphasis is placed on how the role player felt during the role play and why. Players are encouraged to surface feelings which occurred as a result of the behavior of other role players during the enactment. For example: "How did you feel when John said that he postponed the appointment he had made with you?" Or, "How did you feel when Mary crossed her arms and tightened her hands during the interview?" Much of the discussion is focused on the specific ways role players communicate and how that communication affects others.

Role players may also be encouraged to share any insights they may have gained about themselves which occurred during the role play. Also, group members are encouraged to express feelings that may have been triggered by things that occurred during the role play.

Some developmental role plays do not place as much emphasis on surfacing feelings, attitudes, and motivation. In these cases, the person "on the hot seat" may be required to apply and integrate a variety of concepts previously learned, such as problem-solving methods, counseling techniques, and/or decision-making procedures. The post-enactment discussion questions then will focus on issues related to these subjects.

As indicated earlier, the developmental role play can be used to test different approaches and solutions to problem situations. For example, the productivity and motivation of a long-term employee have dropped dramatically in recent years, despite repeated constructive efforts by management to aid the employee in improving his or her work. A management decision has now been made to request the employee to accept early retirement—something the employee is known to be resisting. A group could agree upon how this interview might be conducted and, in the post-enactment discussion, modification in the approach might be developed. Or, several participants could try out their approaches in a group setting, and then it might be possible to decide upon which approach would be the best one for actually dealing with the employee.

If an observer guide is used in the role play, the trainer may base his or her class discussions on the guide. Typical observer sheet questions might include:

1. Who did most of the talking?
2. What communication approaches seemed to be particularly effective?
3. Did body language give us any clues on how the interviewer felt about the interviewee?
4. What kind of eye contact took place between the interviewer and the interviewee?
5. Was a decision reached—and if so, what was it?

Summary

The common elements required for success in both method-centered and developmental role playing have to do with (1) identifying an area where the trainee feels a need for training and/or generating trainee motivation related to that need, (2) sustaining a climate of trust, (3) anticipating and dealing with possible trainee anxiety related to the role-playing situation, (4) providing trainees with feedback on both the content of the enactment and the attitude projected by the role players, and (5) providing the feedback on the content and attitude so that each is clearly distinguished in the post-enactment discussion.

By way of a visual summary, Figure 1 may assist you in understanding the steps a designer/trainer must go through before conducting the role-play session. This figure will, as well, help to keep you oriented to the detailed discussion which follows in the Design Format chapter. You may wish to refer back to this chart as the need arises.

Figure 1

The Role-Play Process

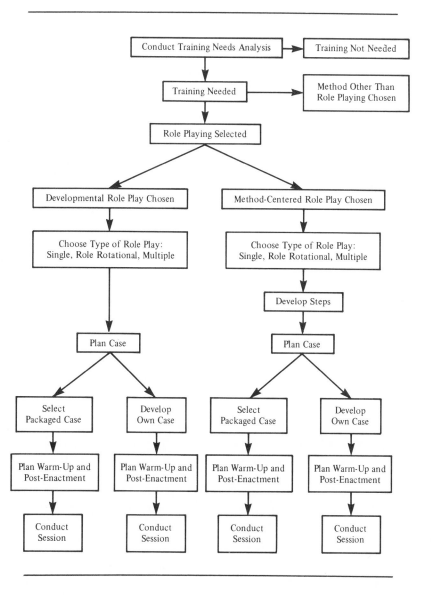

III.

DESIGN FORMAT

Introduction

In this chapter, we will first discuss the relationship of training objectives to the choice of training methods. We will then describe the three basic types of role-playing enactments. This will be followed by a full discussion of the three sequential steps that take place in all role-playing sessions: (a) the warm-up, (b) the enactment, and (c) the post-enactment discussion.

Training Objectives

We will begin the chapter by discussing the key choices that the trainer needs to make *prior* to both planning the session and carrying out the session. Without this type of analysis, the effectiveness of the session will be seriously lessened. We begin then with objectives.

Objectives determine the direction the trainer takes in planning any type of training effort. Typically, training programs are developed because (1) there is a need for some skill training, (2) there is a lack of knowledge in some area, and training appears to be a means of imparting the information, or (3) there is a need to modify or influence certain trainee attitudes or sensitize them to specific issues or concerns. In each of these situations, a training effort may be helpful, but the methods employed and the design of the program will be different.

To start, the trainer performs a needs analysis based on verifiable data, and asks these questions: (1) does this lack of skill, information, or attitude problem really exist; and (2) how important is it to the organization that "it" is handled? Assuming the answer to the first is "yes" and to the second "very," a trainer proceeds to dissect the problem more carefully in an attempt to determine the most appropriate means of handling it. This dissection involves determining whether there are skill deficiencies or an attitude problem. Sometimes, problems involve all three. But in order to design an effective training instrument, a breakdown is required. Even if several areas are problems, each one has to be dealt with separately. For example, managers may have problems dealing with women and minorities appearing in management or sales positions. These same managers may lack knowledge of Equal Employment Opportunity laws and guidelines. The trainer is confronted with both a knowledge problem and an attitude/skill problem. One intervention might be designed to handle the lack of knowledge using a lecture format, and another intervention might be designed to handle the attitude/skill problem using role playing.

For problems that involve a skill deficiency or an attitude/awareness deficiency, role playing would be an appropriate choice. As indicated in Chapter I, trainers rate role playing as a *preferred choice* for these types of problems.

The next step is to determine which specific type of role play—method-centered or developmental—is to be used. Here, the trainer needs to go from a determination of what the problem is to specifically what needs to be achieved. Once we know what the problem is, the next step is to decide what specifically has to happen in order to judge the training effort a success. We know the group cannot complete a new sales call effectively. After the training program, what do we want this group to know, sense, feel, be able to do, etc., that is different from pre-training? The answer to *that* question will determine if method-centered or developmental role play is a better vehicle. In other words, depending on what the outcome needs to be, one makes a choice.

Guidelines for Choosing a Method-Centered
or Developmental Role Play

1. If there is a need to get people to learn an interactive skill and that skill can be *analyzed* simply and put into a series of *simple, clear steps,* use method-centered role playing. For example:

- how to initiate a sales call; or
- how to handle an irate customer; or
- how to conduct a job interview.

2. If there is a need to create awareness or bring issues to the surface, use developmental role play to integrate previous learning. For example:

- A group of management trainees has taken three theory courses on decision-making, interpersonal communications, and problem-solving. Put them in a selection interviewing situation where they are faced with two candidates of similar quality.
- Have health care personnel role play interactions with "patients" to gain insight into this unique interaction.
- Have counselors role play with "troubled students" to learn how better to deal with typical problems faced on the job.

Once the choice is made to use method-centered or developmental role play, the trainer can determine specifics, such as whether to use single or multiple role play, what types of warm-ups are best, and other issues relevant to the format. The remainder of the chapter describes the types of role play and the parts of the session. This information will guide the trainer in designing the specific session.

Types of Role-Playing Enactments

We have described two basic types of role playing. Both may utilize written cases, but method-centered role plays always have guidelines or steps preset for the trainees to follow, while developmental role plays allow (encourage, really) trainees to develop a case as they see fit, and then to gain insight from that experience.

The decision to use single, role rotational, or multiple role play for the enactment depends on the objectives of the group and the leader. The descriptions that follow for each of these types will help the trainer in that choice.

Single Role Play

Single role playing involves two or three people doing a role play in front of the group. It is commonly used by many trainers and is ideally suited to several types of situations. The basic reason to use single role play would be to create awareness of an attitudinal issue that needs discussion and thought. By having people come to the front of the class and act out a conflict situation, attitudes and issues come to the surface. People become aware of issues, discuss them, and look for solutions. A second use of a single role play may be to give the group one common experience to draw upon. For example, the role play is part of a problem-solving session, and everyone needs to see and hear the same information to analyze the quality of the decision made and how it was decided. Or, the trainer may wish to make a point about different perceptions and want to expose people to a common stimulus in order to demonstrate how perceptions vary.

The fact that everyone in the group is seeing the same interaction and focusing on a common experience is one of the key advantages of single role play. The class can then analyze together all the dynamics of the role play. The trainer's role is somewhat simplified because all the energy is focused on one interaction. The post-enactment discussion centers on that one interaction and can be more in-depth.

There are, of course, disadvantages. One of the disadvantages is that people in the role play might feel embarrassed being up in front of the class. There is no doubt that they are on display and will be subject to analysis. If the group is very cohesive and supportive, this may not be a problem, but if this is not the case, difficulties will undoubtedly arise. Another disadvantage is that if the players do an inadequate job of handling the role play, they may be subject to negative feedback. Unless the trainer is very careful, this could lead to defensiveness on the part of the role players. Another limitation of the single role play is that only *one* person has an opportunity to practice a skill. This is because in the standard role play all the participants except one act as a foil to that one person attempting to solve a problem. Norman Maier's term for this is "sitting in the hot seat." Therefore, trainers who desire to give trainees actual practice in implementation skills should give greater consideration to using multiple or role rotational role play, as both of these types of role plays allow for a large proportion of the class members to play "hot seat" roles.

Role Rotational Role Play

In role rotational role play, another form of the single role play, several different pairs or triads have an opportunity to come to the front of the group and handle a given problem. One advantage of this method is that, like the single role play, it focuses attention on one interaction at a time. Because several different individuals are trying, the embarrassment issue is less of a problem.

In role rotational role play, one player becomes the foil; then a series of other role players are designated by the trainer to attempt to deal with the problem or situation. For example, one class member becomes a poorly motivated

employee who must be talked to by a manager with the
objective of achieving improved employee performance.
Then, in sequence, two, three, or four different "managers"
will attempt to identify the problem and deal with the
employee's poor motivation.

If a trainer is trying to have the group develop guidelines
for handling a problem, it is a good method, since, after
several approaches, the best elements will stand out as the
framework that should be used to handle the problem
successfully. Because many people are role playing, no one
individual is being analyzed at length. The emphasis shifts to
the problem, where it belongs.

A second advantage is that this method dramatically
demonstrates how the same problem is approached by
different people, and that no one style is necessarily the best,
since different styles may very often lead to effective
solutions to the same problem.

There are some disadvantages to using the role rotational
method. As with single role play, the practice is limited to a
few people. Again, the post-enactment discussion can become
difficult if one person is clearly "the worst" in handling the
problem.

Multiple Role Play

In multiple role play, the entire class is given a chance to
participate. The class is broken into groups of two or three,
and everyone is given a part to play or an observer guide to
help give feedback to the others in the small group. This type
of situation is obviously a "natural" when the trainer wants
everyone (or almost everyone) to have an opportunity to
practice.

Multiple role plays are used to develop skills in problem-
solving and decision-making, as well as in interpersonal
communications. They are often used to "warm-up" trainees
to other role-playing experiences. Since it is not done in front

of the entire class, role playing in small groups presents a minimal threat to the trainees.

As with single role playing, there are advantages and disadvantages. The advantages include (1) allowing all members of the group to participate actively, (2) demonstrating that many different styles of solving a dilemma can be successful, and (3) eliminating the embarrassment of performing in front of a large group of people.

Allowing people to participate can be especially important if the trainer is teaching a new skill or behavior. Practice is a part of the learning process and critical if people need to learn how to do something. The idea of demonstrating different styles may or may not be relevant to a particular lesson. For example, if one is training people to handle a standard interaction, like a check-out at a car rental agency, he or she may want to encourage a more standard style. On the other hand, the training session may involve learning to handle a discrimination complaint. Because the interaction is both longer and more complex, different styles would be used and possibly encouraged. It would also seem likely that practice would help the trainees. In that case, multiple role play would be of benefit to both in terms of giving people practice and pointing out the possibility of different styles. There is no doubt that the third factor—eliminating embarrassment—is helpful in any case. However, using multiple role play only because it decreases embarrassment is not recommended.

It would seem to us that using multiple role play to surface different perspectives to a problem and/or develop different solutions is a sound reason to use the format. It might be used as a catalyst to discuss the different ways that people "see" a problem and attempt to solve it. Since it is a more subtle training technique, the trainer would need to be clear about what was to be achieved.

These advantages can help the trainer to point out some

key factors. Practicing and doing are essential to becoming proficient at something. Since people will be in a position to practice, they will quickly realize that they *do need* to practice. Their own struggle will help them see the need to understand the dynamics of what is happening in interpersonal communications. They will sense that actually handling a situation is a good deal more difficult than intellectualizing about it. Also, the trainer will be able to point out in the post-enactment discussion how various styles can be used to solve problems. People, given the same information, will handle it differently because they "see" it differently.

The disadvantages of multiple role play are that (1) there may be little time for discussion of the "process experiences" of each small group, since the process discussions of what happened in role play are of limited interest to the entire group; (2) a group may finish considerably before or after the others and be left waiting; and (3) since the group has had different experiences with various degrees of success, it becomes more difficult in the post-enactment discussion to pull the discussion together in a sensible, cohesive way.

All three types of enactment are useful. As noted, all have distinct advantages and disadvantages. The trainer needs to analyze objectives carefully so that the choice of methods maximizes results.

Functional Phases of Role-Playing Sessions

The typical role-playing session, whether developmental or method-centered, involves three distinct functional phases: (1) the warm-up, (2) the enactment, and (3) the post-enactment discussion. All have a purpose and are interdependent.

The Warm-Up

A group needs to get "warmed up" before starting an actual role play. The primary objective of the warm-up is to get the trainees to participate in a productive way in the role-play experience. In the warm-up, the trainer needs to deal with two key areas: First, there is a need to help the trainees to understand the reason for the role play—to get excited about it and see its appropriateness. Second, the trainer needs to handle the possible anxiety of the trainees. Certain group members may feel worried about exposure or appearing less than adequate in front of a group. These fears are real and need to be taken into consideration.

Warm-ups for method-centered role plays are generally more structured and precise. The warm-up in a method-centered role play is really an opportunity to explain the principles behind the method. The warm-up has two tasks—developing motivation *and* teaching a method of handling a task or a type of problem.

The key steps of the method-centered role play are introduced and discussed in the warm-up. The steps should be outlined and classified. Any questions that trainees have regarding the steps should be answered at this time. An example of key steps for handling a subordinate who has a work motivation problem is given below:

1. State problem in terms of performance deficiency (not behavior deficiency).
2. Request subordinate's assistance in resolving the problem and discuss both your view and his or hers on how to achieve a performance improvement.
3. Arrive at an agreement as to a course of action.
4. Decide on a follow-up date to discuss progress.

In developmental role-play sessions, the warm-up involves less planning but a high level of interpersonal skill. In these sessions, trainees are going to be put in situations that require them to experiment with handling a problem; e.g., your subordinate has recently encountered a severe domestic problem and has requested a counseling session with you to discuss how it is affecting his or her work and his or her future in the organization. Issues focused on will be attitudes, feelings, and techniques. Since no preset guidelines are given, the trainees are more likely to go far afield. Simply, the developmental role play puts people in a more open-ended and possibly vulnerable position. In order to decrease trainee anxiety, the trainer would need to develop a level of trust and group cohesiveness that may not be as necessary in a method-centered situation. The warm-up for developmental role plays, then, is really more for motivational and "relaxation" purposes, rather than focusing on principles.

There are several ways that a trainer can reduce the anxiety of trainees. First, the trainer should explain carefully the objectives of the role-playing session. This will help relax training novices, who may feel the session is designed more to reveal flaws than to build skills. Have everyone introduce himself or herself. Saying a few words about themselves is another step that should be done. A role-playing session is a group effort and as such requires that people feel at ease with each other. Ensuring that there is privacy and quiet is also key. Trainees may begin to feel relaxed with the group, but if they worry about other people possibly dropping by, it may cause tensions to build.

Specifically, the warm-up can consist of discussion group exercises and other techniques that emphasize the problem to be handled in the role play and the enactment. It should in some way emphasize to the trainee how critical it is to learn how to handle this problem area effectively.

Let's assume that the role-playing enactment will involve handling a discipline situation from the supervisor's viewpoint. An appropriate warm-up might be having the group discuss how this problem is usually handled, their own experiences and feelings about discipline interviews, and what they feel are the problem areas. This type of discussion accomplishes the purposes of the role-play warm-up noted— namely, it serves to lower anxiety, since members of the group will tend to reinforce each other and support each other in a discussion about common problems; and, secondly, it will motivate the members to participate in the role play, since it will be clear that the problem exists and must be handled.

It should be stressed again that warm-ups should be used to point out the *job-relatedness* of a problem. If trainees do not really believe that the problem is relevant, they will not fully participate on the level necessary to acquire skills. Typical kinds of problems used in warm-ups are: How does one deal with an employee complaint about bad working conditions? Which problems occur in responding to an irate customer? How does one deal with a student who would like more information about a variety of courses? How does one deal with difficult patients in a hospital setting?

If the problem to be handled in the role-play sessions is new to the trainees or different from their common experiences—i.e., learning a new skill—a reading assignment or viewing of a film might be very productive. Often, trainees need information to handle the interpersonal problem effectively. Clearly written or audio-visual materials are sound choices for these warm-ups.

In the Appendix are six examples of complete role plays, each with a warm-up exercise. These examples will clarify the purpose. The point is that every session needs some degree of warm-up. The trainer should analyze the group before the session to determine how much or little is needed before the role playing can become productive.

A note about group size. Generally speaking, role playing should not be done in groups which exceed 20 or 25 participants. When role plays are conducted in front of the class (as in single role playing and role rotational role playing), a large-size group will often tend to intimidate some role players. Also, it is more difficult to build trust levels in large groups as compared to smaller groups. However, in multiple role playing, since there is no exposure to an observing group, class size can be somewhat larger than the 25.

Ideally, the room will be comfortable and unclassroom-like. Chairs should be easily movable and initially set up in a circle or U-shape to facilitate discussion. The trainer should be open and relaxed. If the trainer is overly formal or rigid, the role-playing session will reflect this. By the same token, if the trainer makes it appear that the role playing isn't too serious a matter, that attitude will also be picked up. The point is to relax people but also to get them to understand the relevance of role playing.

Selecting Role Players. Enactments need participants. Inform participants of the number of roles in the case. Ask for volunteers to play before or after the roles are described. Wait at least 20 seconds before you give up on getting a volunteer. In almost all cases, people will volunteer for the role. If this procedure does not work, choose people who retain eye contact with you. If no one does this, pick people from the group. If possible select those who are:

    (1) verbal,

    (2) animated,

    (3) articulate (as demonstrated in class discussion), and

    (4) not overly anxious.

After you have obtained people from the class to play the roles, ask them to study their parts a few minutes. The rest of the group can simultaneously be briefed on how to appropriately use the observer guide (if one exists).

The above guidelines pertain to single and role rotational role playing. In multiple role playing, roles are simply assigned (see page 109). This is usually done by having the class count off in A's, B's, C's, etc., each letter designating a role, or an observer.

The Enactment

The enactment stage of role-playing sessions involves

actually doing the role plays; it is slightly different in the two basic types of sessions—method-centered and developmental. See the Appendix for enactment examples.

Method-Centered Role-Play Enactments. The trainer should follow the procedures below:

1. The trainer informs the group that enactment is about to start. The trainer should go over one more time the key steps or procedures that the role players are to follow.

2. The trainer then describes the situation (possibly referring to a general information sheet). Regardless of whether single, role rotational, or multiple role plays will be used, the trainer should read the situation aloud.

3. Those persons who will be involved in the role playing should be given briefing sheets which describe their role. Examples of briefing sheets are to be found in the sample role plays included in the Appendix.

4. All persons who will not be involved directly in the role play should be given observer guides. If observer guides are not available for the case, copies of the role-play briefing sheets should be handed out.

5. While the trainees are reading over their briefing sheets or observer guides, the trainer should be nearby to answer any questions or clarify any issues.

6. The trainer now instructs the role players to come to the front of the group (in the case of the single role play) or to get ready to begin by positioning their chairs (as in the case of the multiple role play).

7. To begin the role play, the trainer sets the scene by identifying the characters in the role play. Then the trainer starts the action by describing how the scene is about to begin. For example, "Lee Baker, the supervisor, has just called Bob into the office to discuss the situation."

Developmental Role-Play Enactments. In conducting an enactment for a developmental role-playing session, the trainer follows these key points:

1. The trainer tells the group that the enactment part of the role-playing session is beginning.

2. The trainer states the goals of the role plays—usually, to gain insight into how and why the interaction is occurring the way it is (i.e., process) and to gain insight into how a situation like the one about to happen can be handled most effectively.

3. The trainer describes the situation the trainees are about to role play. The trainer informs the group whether single role, role rotational, or multiple role plays will be used.

4. Those persons who will be involved in the role playing should be given briefing sheets which describe their particular roles.

5. Those persons who will not be directly involved in the role play should ideally be given observer guides to use while watching the role plays. These observer guides will help center their attention on the important elements in the role play.

6. While the trainees are reading over their briefing sheets or observer guides, the trainer should be nearby to answer any questions or clarify any problems raised.

7. The trainer now instructs the role players to come to the front of the group (in the case of the single role play) or to get ready to begin by positioning their chairs (as in the case of the multiple role play).

8. To begin the role play, the trainer sets the scene by restating the identity of the roles being enacted and making a brief statement about what has just happened as the action begins. For example, "Anne Brown, the manager, has just invited Dave into her office to discuss what happened. . . ."

The primary difference between method-centered and developmental role playing is in the goals of the sessions. In the method-centered situation, the goal is to have the trainees learn the *steps or guidelines.* In the case of the developmental role play, the goal is *to gain insights into the process* (motivations and attitudes) of the enactment in order to develop guidelines or helpful ideas about how to behave in similar situations. Or, the goal may be to integrate and apply previous learning to an action situation. In the case of the method-centered role play, the trainees are practicing a skill by enacting the role play. In the developmental situation, the trainees are trying to discover principles and develop insights they can apply in later situations.

Length of Enactments. The time taken for the enactment portion of the role-play session can vary considerably. Most written role plays dealing with communications problems are designed to take eight to 12 minutes. If the case is more complicated and involves a great deal of problem-solving, it can take considerably longer. In a single role-play enactment, the length of one role play done by one group determines the length of the enactment. In a multiple role play, time varies depending on the type of case. Problem-solving cases usually take longer than communications skills role plays. In a role rotational situation, the total enactment part of the session can be longer, since different individuals are given an opportunity to come to the front of the class and try the role play. The trainer needs to determine how much time can and should be spent in the actual enactment. Time must be left for the post-enactment discussion, since it is in that part of the session that the learning is established; and in the case of method-centered role play, reinforced.

In a multiple role-play situation, the trainer is not focusing attention on just one area. Because many role plays are going on simultaneously, the trainer has to walk around the room and listen in to the various groups to see how things are going. The trainer needs data for the post-enactment discussion and for judging how much longer the actual enactment will take. When the trainer notices that groups are beginning to end, a two- or three-minute warning should be given.

Role-Playing Interventions. In general, there are five situations in which the trainer may need to intervene in an enactment. These include dealing with role players who: (1) depart from a role; (2) burlesque their role; (3) perform poorly; (4) need to gain insight into their own behavior or into other people's situations; or (5) become repetitive and prolong the enactment. The following will briefly describe how to deal with each of these situations.

Dealing with Role Players who "Depart" the Role: In some cases, a role player will attempt to "discuss" his or her role rather than play it. In effect, he or she might say, "Well, if I were the supervisor in this case, I would say. . . ." In effect, they attempt to play their role in the third person. This is normally caused by trainee anxiety of, in effect, being in the "hot seat." Talking about what one *would* do is normally easier than actually *doing* it for some trainees. If this occurs, it will tend only to be at the beginning of a role play. The trainer should simply say something along the following line: "John, you are the person you are talking about. Stay in the role and act as if you were actually handling the situation now." Said clearly and firmly, this will normally get the role player into his or her role.

Dealing with Burlesquing the Role: Occasionally, a role player will burlesque the role playing, acting it so broadly or humorously that he or she cannot be taken seriously. This, like the role player who wants to depart from the role, is normally caused by trainee anxiety. The problem normally can easily be handled by the trainer. He or she intervenes and asks the role player to play the role *naturally.* Example: "Terry, I'm sure you would not play your part this way in a real situation. I'm going to ask you to play this role as you would *really* handle it. Play it *naturally."*

Dealing with the Poorly Performing Role Player: In most

cases, when a role player is ineffective in handling his or her role, the trainer will allow the role play to come to completion. However, in some cases, the role player does so badly that he or she may be adversely affected by the experience unless the trainer intervenes. This situation takes skill and tact on the part of the trainer. One way to handle this situation is to call a time out and ask the role player who is having difficulty (allowing the player time to respond to each one): (1) How well do you think you are doing? (2) What do you think the problem is? (3) What change in your approach might help things go better? Typically, this will help the person reevaluate how he or she is doing and proceed more effectively.

If this approach is unsuccessful because the role player is having difficulty assessing how to react properly, the trainer can ask the class to come up with a solution. This can come about by asking the role player's permission to tap the class as a problem-solving group. The trainer then asks the class questions that are closely related to those asked of the role player previously. (1) What do you see as the problem? (2) Can you think of more useful approaches for solving it? Usually, the player will react positively to their suggestions and proceed on a different path. The class approach is particularly helpful because, when successful, it provides the player with effective problem-solving techniques. Even if it fails, the role player will not feel on the spot because he or she was just trying to follow the class's advice.

Aiding a Role Player Gain Insight into His or Her Own Behavior: At times in a developmental role play, which is focused on developing personal growth and insight, and *only* in this type of role play, it is desirable to intervene when it is clear one of the role players has little awareness of the impact his or her behavior is having on the other person. For example, the role player may be overly aggressive or hostile. When this occurs, the trainer may want to create a situation where the role player can become aware of the consequences of this approach in dealing with others. This can be done by using a technique known as *role reversal.*

In role reversal, the trainer has the role players change roles. In this case, for example, the manager, in the middle of the enactment, changes roles with his or her subordinate. This also means that role players must physically change places with each other. After the manager, for example, has learned how it really feels to have been on the receiving end, the trainees again reverse roles, with the enactment played out in such a way that both role players end up playing their original roles.

Role reversal might be used in the following situation. A person playing the role of a social worker has just become very hostile and abrasive to a client. At that moment, the trainer might want to say, "O.K., Laura, you now become Mr. Miller, your client, and John, you become Miss Atkins, the social worker." After the enactment has gone long enough for Laura to get some idea of how it feels to be on the receiving end of her own behavior as a social worker—perhaps three to five minutes—roles are again reversed and the role play is brought to a completion.

It should be pointed out that role reversal intervention requires great sensitivity and skill and should only be undertaken after the trainer has had substantial experience with role playing.

Dealing with Repetitive Role Plays: In general, it is best to let role plays come to a conclusion naturally. If the same points are being made repetitively, the trainer might say something like, "I feel we have covered the main points, so let's stop here and discuss what has occurred so far."

Observer Guides

Experience demonstrates that trainers often have a problem separating content issues from process issues in the post-enactment discussion. Because of this frequent failure, participants are left confused about what they were supposed to have learned from the role-play session. In order to eliminate or minimize this problem, it is helpful to structure questions that will separate these issues. A helpful way to do that is to create and use an observer guide. Questions for the guide (whether content or process) should relate directly to objectives set forth by the trainer. Generally, one should deal with content questions first, then process issues.

An observer guide can be distributed to participants to use during the enactment or designed just for the trainer to structure the post-enactment discussion. In either case, it should be written in conjunction with the case to insure that the post-enactment discussion is clearly targeted.

For Method-Centered Role Plays. In the case of the method-centered role play, the observer guide should consist primarily of questions related to the key steps or guidelines. In other words, the observer should be watching to see if the guidelines are being followed. If they are not being followed, there should be questions that help the observer note why the person is not following the steps. Is the person refusing to listen, for example? Observer guides for method-centered role plays can also involve questions about the process—i.e., how did the manager handle the defensiveness of the other manager? One note of caution: too many questions can be as bad as too few. Try to determine what the important elements are and limit your questions accordingly. In the case of a method-centered role play, the critical focus should be on the key steps.

For Developmental Role Plays. Though observer guides are frequently used in method-centered role playing, they are used less often in developmental role playing. However, they provide a valuable learning experience for class participants and can be used in conjunction with most developmental role plays.

Writing observer guides for developmental role plays is somewhat more difficult, since the goals are often less clear. The questions should cover *both* process and content. Remember that this method is being used to determine effective and non-effective ways of handling a problem situation. Questions should all help elicit that information. For example: list the three things that you feel helped the interview run effectively.

The Post-Enactment Discussion

The purpose of the post-enactment discussion is connected to the purpose of the enactment. In the case of method-centered role playing, the purpose of the enactment is to apply the steps or guidelines outlined in the warm-up and to see how they work to handle a problem situation or an interpersonal interaction effectively. The post-enactment discussion in this case centers on whether the steps were followed, why and/or why not, and reinforcement of those behaviors used that were in line with the steps or guidelines. This is not to imply that the entire post-enactment discussion will be a matter of yes/no questions concerning steps. There will be discussion of broader process issues and attitudinal areas which will develop naturally. Examples of how post-enactment discussions are to be conducted can be found in the Appendix.

Giving Feedback. * The critical learning of most role-playing experiences comes in the post-enactment discussion, where the trainer attempts to crystallize the significance of the role plays for the class. If the feedback is formulated by the trainer or by participants in a way that is hurtful, or too pointed, or threatening, it will often lead to defensiveness or hostility, and the role players will reject the feedback. Below

*The authors wish to acknowledge the contribution of Mal Shaw, upon whose ideas these feedback guidelines are based.

are four rules to follow in giving feedback. Use of these guidelines is particularly important when personal behavior is being reviewed.

Feedback Should Be Descriptive, Not Evaluative: Whether one is asking someone to give feedback on a technical issue (such as a discussion relating to the quality of a decision made during the course of a role play) or on personal behavior, it is more desirable to encourage descriptive rather than evaluative feedback. For example, a group might review performance by saying: "That was a lousy job," or "Sam Smith doesn't do a good job of discussing performance factors." These are both evaluative comments. Rather, the discussion leader should encourage people to describe what happened. In the same situation, a descriptive piece of feedback might be: "I notice during the interview that on several occasions the subordinate seemed confused." Notice that although the statement implies that the interview wasn't well handled, the feedback describes an actual occurrence as seen by the observer. Confusion may have resulted from any number of things, but there is less emphasis on blaming the interviewer.

Feedback Which Deals with Human Factors Should Generally Be Expressed in Terms of the Observer's Own Experience Rather Than Someone Else's: For example, rather than saying, "I think Sandy did a poor job of handling that sales interview," it is more effective if the observer says, "I have been in situations just like the one Sandy was in, and they tend to make me feel uncomfortable. I recognize that I don't always do a good job of making my points." Thus, the feedback tends to be less directed at one individual, and others can begin sharing their own experiences.

Feedback Should Not Be Dogmatic or Overgeneralized: For example, in an employment interview role play, one type of feedback might be, "The interviewer talked too much and needs to change his interviewing technique." This comment is evaluative and tends to be dogmatic. More acceptable feedback would be, "There were times when I recognized that as an interviewer I might be giving the applicant a lot of information early in the game, but I wonder whether we shouldn't spend more time drawing the person out. How do others feel?" The second approach is less evaluative, tends to seek the opinions of others, and is not personally critical of the interviewer in the role play.

Feedback Should Not Assign Motives or Make Judgments About Underlying Attitudes: One example that has been used frequently involves several individuals standing in a line, one of whom steps on the toes of another. The injured party might say, "You're trying to hurt me," or "You're trying to push me out of line." Thus, he or she would make judgments about the motives of the other person. These might be totally unjustified and lead to misunderstanding and hostility. He or she could, on the other hand, respond by saying, "You stepped on my toe," which describes the incident but does not assign motives or values.

Similarly, in giving feedback on role playing, it is generally better to describe what happened. After watching a role play, one could say, "One of the participants seemed to talk quite a bit more than the others. I had the feeling that he was pushing for a specific goal." This would be somewhat descriptive and tentative. On the other hand, an observer might say, "One of the group members is trying to take over the group and wants to be boss, and he doesn't care how other people feel." This latter feedback is evaluative, assigns motives, and might block discussion.

In other words, as a participant in a role play, it is generally easier for people to accept descriptive, non-evaluative feedback such as, "Well, Lee, you talked quite a bit during that meeting," than it is to accept a statement such as, "Well, Sam, it is clear you were trying to take over and you didn't care whose toes you stepped on." Clearly, the second kind of feedback could lead to disagreement, hostility, and a difficult learning experience.

It should be noted that there are situations in which direct and evaluative feedback is appropriate, but this is usually true when there is a skilled trainer or psychologist to guide the group and when there is sufficient time to work through the various areas of difference or hostility.

In a developmental role play, the post-enactment discussion is more complicated in nature, since it is based on the idea of discovery-oriented learning. Therefore, the responsibility for having the group bring out insights and develop principles rests with the trainer. The trainer needs to guide the group through a series of carefully thought out questions to "discover" the relevant points learned during the enactment.

Examples of questions that can be used in post-enactment discussions for developmental role plays include: (1) For a session geared to helping managers improve their communications skills—What behaviors did the manager use that helped relax the employee? (2) For a session designed to help supervisors assess their own level of competence and self-assurance with problem-solving—How did you feel you handled the problem? What information do you think would have helped you make an even better solution? (3) For a session designed to help people integrate a large range of subject matter and apply it to on-the-job situations—How well do you think the manager handled all aspects of the problem with the employee? Did he or she concentrate only on one aspect of the problem? For further examples, see the Appendix examples and Developing Observer Guides in the Developmental Guide chapter.

In each of the three types of enactments, there are various types of post-enactment discussions that have been found to be particularly helpful. Each is described as follows:

Single Role-Play Post-Enactment Discussion. The key

point to remember when having a post-enactment discussion with a single role play is the importance of beginning the discussion with the person who was "in the hot seat." This person has been on display during the enactment. It would be well to ask that person how he or she felt the role play went and upon what good points or bad points did he or she want to comment. This person is being given an opportunity to explain what he or she did and why he or she did it; and it gives the individual a chance to decompress.

The next person who would be given time to comment on the role play is the one who acted in the foil role. If there are more than one 'foil' roles, each of the people should be given an opportunity to explain his or her position. These people can be asked questions about how they reacted to certain behaviors, if they felt the issue was resolved in a fair or understanding way, and how they might have handled it.

Only after the players have had an opportunity to react to the role play should other members of the group be brought in to the discussion. At this point, the observer guides should serve as the basis for the discussion. The trainer is there to reinforce key steps (as learned in method-centered role play) or to guide the discussion to analyze general principles that can be learned from the experience.

Role Rotational Role-Play Post-Enactment Discussion. As with single role play and multiple role play, the post-enactment discussion for method-centered and developmental role-play sessions vary slightly. In the case of method-centered role play, the discussion would be concerned primarily with how the role players used different styles to follow a common set of guidelines or steps—*emphasis being on the steps which were followed, not the steps which were omitted.* Again, the observer guide is used as a focal point. The use of role rotational role play could generate some very positive discussion, since it would demonstrate the large variety of possible styles.

In a developmental, role rotational role play, the post-enactment discussion centers on how the individuals (typically two to five) rotated the roles and handled the situation. The emphasis should not center on the specific people but rather on the general learning that evolved from different people trying to deal with and experience the same situation. The discussion can be generated and organized around key questions, such as—What effective behaviors did you see used by all of the individuals? What behaviors might you have used that no one used? Why would you have done so? What types of things in general do you feel are not helpful in handling situations of this type? These questions can help focus attention on the problem to be solved and the trainer objectives. Other, more specific questions related to other trainer objectives can be referred to. These questions would be specified on the observer guides which may have been used during the enactment.

Multiple Role-Play Post-Enactment Discussion. In multiple role play for a method-centered role-play session, the trainer would collect data from each of the observers. A common data base, from different observers, should be possible, provided they all have based their individual feedback on the observer guide used for the case. Since the emphasis in method-centered role play is on following steps, the data would consist primarily of how well people did or did not follow the guidelines. The discussion would revolve around three areas: (1) how well did people do who followed the steps; (2) the effect the steps had in the role-play enactment; and (3) any problems that occurred in attempting to follow the steps. The trainer uses the discussion to *reinforce* the steps by emphasizing, through points raised by the observers, how the steps serve the needs of handling a problem situation effectively and efficiently.

If multiple role play is used with a developmental session, the discussion centers on the specific emphasis the trainer has built into the observer guide. That is, the trainer has determined to achieve certain key objectives related to skill integration, assessment, or process skills of some type. The observer guide is designed to have people focus in on certain behaviors or attitudes related to the objectives. As in method-centered multiple role play, a data roundup is used. Here are some examples of questions which might be included: (1) For a session designed to demonstrate multiple styles of problem-solving—What was the solution reached? How was the solution arrived at?; or (2) For a session designed to assess strengths in integrating and applying information and knowledge—How well do you feel you handled all the aspects of the problem? Which areas did you overlook—or need to consider in greater depth? The informa- tion gathered can be summarized on the chalkboard or on charts. This feedback helps the entire group achieve the objectives of the trainer.

Videotapes and Post-Enactment Discussion. Videotape is sometimes used in role-playing sessions. Despite the amount of attention this has received in training publications, its actual practice is limited. The purpose of using videotape in role-playing sessions is to provide more complete feedback for the people participating. It makes recall easier and can affect behavior change more quickly.

When people can see what they are doing, they can correct any mistakes more easily. The key element involved in the use of videotape feedback is creating a supportive climate. Because a video feedback session can be very revealing and put people in an uncomfortable position, the trainer needs to be certain that the group is cohesive and supportive before using it. Also, it requires that the trainer explain carefully to the trainees exactly why the tape is being used. The trainees need to feel comfortable with the setup and be clear on how it will help them in learning new skills or gaining insight in their behavior.

In the Appendix are three examples of method-centered role-play sessions and three examples of developmental role-play sessions. Each helps to clarify and exemplify design characteristics of a role-play session.

IV.

OUTCOMES

Introduction

In the preceding chapters, we have described role playing and its various uses. We have discussed in detail the different design formats that are possible and given examples of each. As an educator or trainer, your next logical question is: "What will this instructional design do for the student/trainer?" In this chapter, we address ourselves to that question.

Outcomes of Method-Centered Role Plays

In a method-centered role play, the trainer sets out to give the trainee a new set of behaviors. The goal is to have the trainee know how to conduct a specific interaction that he or she did not know how to conduct before the session began. For example, the trainer may have set out to train someone on how to handle a customer complaint. The objective, simply, would be that after the session, the trainee would be able to successfully conduct a meeting with a customer who was making a complaint. To judge the success of the session, one would have to observe persons in these situations during post-training or have customers describe how well the meetings were conducted. Within the session, success could be judged by how well the trainee handled a complaint in a role play after having had an opportunity to try it a few times and discuss what happened. Depending on how realistic the role playing was, the success of the training could be observed.

Behavior modeling is the most structured of the method-centered role-play formats. In this training, the trainees are presented not only with steps or guidelines on how to handle a specific situation, but also are shown a "model" film or videotape which uses the steps presented. After the model is shown, trainees rehearse the guidelines or steps in an attempt to learn the procedure. During the time some trainees are actually rehearsing, others in the group are using guides to observe the action. A post-enactment discussion follows. Behavior modeling has been used in industry and continues to be used with increasing frequency. Research has verified its effectiveness.

Sorcher (1971) was the first to apply behavior modeling in industry. His work at General Electric was evaluated against the goals of his program—to reduce turnover of new employees by helping the new employees develop specific skills that would allow them to adapt to and cope with a job in industry (Burnaska, 1976). The six-month turnover rate of employees not trained was 72 percent. Those individuals who received training and who worked for supervisors who had also been trained had a turnover rate of only 28 percent.

AT&T has done extensive work with behavior modeling in training supervisors. There, a study was done under the direction of Joseph L. Moses, Manager Personnel Research. In this extensive study, described by Moses and Ritchie (1976), 183 supervisors were randomly assigned to training or control groups after being matched by sex, age, department, length of service, and number of subordinates. One group (N=90) received behavior modeling training. The control group (N=93) did not. The results showed that the performance of the trained supervisors was dramatically superior to that of the untrained supervisors. The trained supervisors seem to have improved their skills in a way directly related to the training. Of the trained group, 84 percent of the supervisors were seen to perform "exceptionally well" or "above average" in their handling of the problem discussions. On the other hand, of the untrained supervisors, only 32 percent were rated this way.

General Electric conducted a similar study with 62 middle level managers and a control group of 62 managers. Trained judges who had no knowledge of who was trained consistently rated the trained managers as superior to the untrained.

In an IBM study, employee satisfaction was surveyed at 31 offices. Managers at 18 of these offices then received training. A later survey indicated that employee satisfaction increased at those offices where managers received training.

Behavior modeling is an effective type of method-centered role playing. Based on its success thus far, its popularity is bound to increase. People do learn from imitation, and behavior modeling makes use of social learning theory, combined with role playing, to develop strong training methodology.

Outcomes of Developmental Role Plays

Developmental role plays are designed to help people to modify their behavior by first examining their present behavior. Role plays are done without preset steps or guidelines. People use the role plays to examine how they behave in given situations. Or, given a certain set of circumstances, it is designed to have them act out how they would perceive and act toward a certain person. The trainees in these types of role plays are stepping into roles and then stepping back out of those roles and discovering what took place and why. The goals can vary widely. In all cases, though, the trainees are looking at both content and process with emphasis on the latter. They are examining the feelings, thoughts, and behaviors that came out during the role play.

The point is generally to either learn how other people perceive situations or to determine what types of behaviors do or do not work in given situations.

The outcomes of these role-play sessions depend on several key factors, including the perceptiveness of the trainees and the expertise of the leader/trainer in calling attention to specifics in the role play. It can help people to understand another's feelings and perspective. It can also allow people to experiment with exploring their own behavior by providing a safe environment. For example, an organization may be having problems getting diverse groups, i.e., marketing and production, to see things from each other's viewpoint. A role-playing exercise in which people switch roles could be very effective in reaching the desired outcome of more understanding and communication. Or, a session may be designed to have managers look at the way they communicate with a subordinate in order to seek more effective styles of management. In these types of training sessions, the role of the leader is critical in eliciting insights from the group. As with the structured role-play situation, the post-enactment discussion is critical to achieving stated objectives.

Developmental role plays vary, then, in their uses. In the case of having people look at their own behavior and analyze better means of behaving, the group is really building its own method-centered role play. The means of judging success, i.e., outcomes, are through observation and survey of trainees and peers—or trainees and subordinates. The point is that outcomes can be judged by as many means as are available to the trainee. The key to *achieving* outcomes is careful planning of objectives and post-session evaluation. It should be noted, however, that even a poorly planned role-play session can provide insights to certain people. The trainees, by the very act of participating in a role play, are learning and gaining valuable feedback through the reactions of the group.

We want to emphasize that the single, unique outcome of

role playing is related to the method itself. The basic outcome before any analysis is behavior itself. A role play is a concrete, living event. It is not a theory or an abstraction. It is in its nature to produce a unique outcome—a chance to see and observe human interaction in a controlled, non-threatening environment. This fact, coupled with specific goals, makes it a method whose outcomes are bound to be successful if the session is planned carefully and handled well by the trainer.

Trainee Advantages

Role playing provides students with a unique opportunity to analyze and improve their style, to increase their repertoire of behaviors, or to see things, for a time, through the eyes of another. It can also provide a practice session for experimenting with new behavior styles.

Role playing allows trainees to practice the theory of a subject. The trainees also have the advantage of getting controlled feedback. This feedback about behavior can help them constructively change and/or modify behavior. If the climate is right, trainees can develop skills through practice that would be impractical to learn on the outside. For example, trainees might try two or three different approaches with a new client or problem employee before finding a good fit. By using role play to practice and analyze behavior, they can comfortably initiate the meeting.

Trainer Advantages

The major advantage of role playing as a tool for the trainer is its success in achieving stated objectives and outcomes. You can construct a session using role-play methodology and feel confident that your results will be visible—either in the training itself, or in follow-up measures. Further, role playing provides participation. We are all aware of the importance participation has in keeping interest and motivation high. Also, role playing lifts the burden of sole responsibility for a session from the trainer to a shared responsibility between trainer and trainees. The learning becomes learner-centered and addresses itself to the needs and concerns of the trainee. The trainer, in essence, has the advantage of using one of the few education methods that has proven successful in achieving either behavior change or insight and awareness.

References

Burnaska, R.F. The Effects of Behavior Modeling Training Upon Managers' Behaviors and Employees' Perceptions. *Personnel Psychology,* 1976, *29,* 329-335.

Moses, J.L., and R.J. Ritchie. Supervisory Relationships Training: A Behavioral Evaluation of a Behavior Modeling Program. *Personnel Psychology,* 1976, *29,* 337-343.

Sorcher, M. A Behavior Modification Approach to Supervisory Training. *Professional Psychology,* 1971, *2,* 401-402.

V.

DEVELOPMENTAL GUIDE

The purpose of this chapter is to provide the trainer with a checklist for developing a role-playing session. For each step, the appropriate chapter of this book has been referenced for review. This chapter will clarify and elaborate on certain items in the checklist that were heretofore not covered in detail. Finally, developmental steps are given for method-centered role plays, writing roles for role-playing cases, and developing observer guides. These latter three descriptions, combined with the checklist, should go a long way in helping you develop and implement the role-play instructional design.

A Checklist

1. Determine the objective or objectives of the session. Make certain the objectives point to role playing as a preferred method. See "Training Objectives," Chapter III.
2. Determine whether method-centered or developmental role play would be more appropriate. See "Training Objectives," Chapter III.
3. If a decision is made to use method-centered role play, develop steps or guidelines using this chapter as a reference.
4. Write the role-play case itself. Use remainder of this chapter for help.
5. Determine if single, role rotational, or multiple role play

will be used (see Chapter III) and duplicate sufficient materials for group.

6. Decide whether use of an observer guide is appropriate. If yes, use remainder of this chapter to write guide.
7. Develop warm-up section of the session. Refer to Chapter III, "The Warm-Up," and case examples for guidelines.
8. Prepare for enactment by reviewing all materials and considering how to handle potential problems (see "Role-Playing Interventions," Chapter III).
9. Structure the post-enactment discussion. (Refer to Chapter III, "The Post-Enactment Discussion" and case examples in Appendix, for guidelines.)

Developing Steps for Method-Centered Role Plays

In the case of method-centered role plays, there is a definite need to develop a clear, concise set of guidelines for each interaction being presented. These steps need to be an effective guide to handle a situation.

A trainer can develop steps from three sources: (1) actually observing people successfully completing the interaction, (2) interviewing and discussing the pros and cons of various steps with persons performing the interaction successfully or unsuccessfully, and (3) certain basic communication concepts, such as 'don't interrupt,' 'keep calm,' etc.

An example will illustrate how these three methods can be used to develop an adequate set of steps. Assume a trainer needed to develop a set of steps for handling irate customers who complain about poor service. A study has been done to indicate that this is indeed a frequent problem. The trainer might get a list of service people who handle this problem and begin interviewing them and discussing with them the problems involved, how they successfully handled the situation, where they failed, and so on. He or she might also try to observe certain of these interactions. Finally, using this input, he or she would formulate a series of steps using certain communication guidelines. Before using the steps with a group, the guidelines should be carefully reviewed and perhaps tried out by people in a position to handle such an interaction.

Steps, remember, are in most cases a guideline, *not* a script. The exception might be a service company, like a telephone company that might insist on a consistent, uniform approach to handling and responding to any requests for phone information. This makes sense. This emphasis on the steps as guidelines will make the training more effective and useful. It would give people a skill and provide help without attempting to mold them unnecessarily. The trainer has to write steps broadly, making certain that the behavior necessary is completed but not forced or specifically scripted, i.e.,:

"Greet the person in a friendly way . . ."

NOT

Say—"Oh, did you have a nice weekend?"

The first guides; the second is scripted and too limiting.

The number of steps is another trainer concern. Five to six are generally the average and usually sufficient. More than seven becomes awkward and difficult for the trainee.

A trainer, then, needs to understand the interaction and attempt to structure steps that cover the major components of the interaction. The test is really in the doing. A good trainer is wise to test steps before committing them to final copy.

It is important that the steps a trainer develops are consistent with certain basic communication guidelines. These concepts have been shown to be open, positive communications between individuals. These concepts are:

1. Focus on the problem rather than the person—i.e., do not have a step that would encourage seeking out whom to blame but rather something geared to dealing constructively with the problem or issue at hand.

2. Listen in a responsive manner—i.e., steps should encourage use of techniques which reflect feelings back to the speaker and otherwise encourage two-way communication.

3. Maintain the other person's dignity in an interaction—i.e., steps should always encourage an adult exchange that is geared toward problem-solving; not controlling or manipulating another. Showing the other person respect maintains esteem.

4. Reinforce positive behavior—i.e., steps should encourage being responsible and supportive of those things that are considered positive and desired behavior.

5. Sustain communications—i.e., steps should encourage the continuation of communications beyond the interaction. Specific examples would be the telling of people to call or write if there is any problem, or setting a follow-up date to discuss a situation further. The nature of the interaction dictates the proper communication maintenance.

Writing Roles for Role-Playing Cases

Published role plays which are available in such books as *The Role-Play Technique* and *Using Role Playing in the Classroom* (see Resources, Chapter VI) are worthwhile for developing trainee skills in interpersonal communications and problem-solving. However, the more directly a training group can identify with a particular set of circumstances or more commonly recurring problem, the more likely the group will be motivated to enter role playing actively with interest and motivation. The following description will aid the trainer to write his or her own role-playing case roles based on problems and situations related to the needs of the organization.

Guidelines for Case Effectiveness

Role plays should contain the following elements, if they are to be effective with organizational groups:

(1) have a self-evident relevance to the trainee;

(2) possess clarity;

(3) allow the trainee to identify with the role;

(4) permit role maneuverability;

(5) be sharply focused; and

(6) contain elements of conflict.

Relevance

1. Write problems and situations which are based on elements in the work environment.

2. Use material which has relevance to the trainee's current job or the next position which the trainee may realistically expect to attain.

3. Use terminology and vocabulary which are used by the trainees. Example: If the trainee's primary work has to do with the manufacture of printed circuits, refer to printed circuits, not some abstract model, such as the term "widgets."

Clarity

The trainee usually is expected to read and comprehend the role in three to five minutes. Consequently, the roles should be written as simply as possible. Rapid comprehensibility can be enhanced by giving the case a title that capsulizes the issue, for example, "The Case of the Complaining Customer."

Identifiability

The role should be written to allow the reader to quickly identify with the role. It should be written in the second person with identity created in the first sentence. Example: "You are Tracy Miller, Sales Department Head."

If trainee groups contain both men and women, use "unisex" names for role designation. Example: Terry, Chris, Sandy, Jan, etc.

Role Maneuverability

Roles should be written to permit the role players to deal spontaneously with the situation or problem in their own way. Emphasis should be placed on writing about the situation or problem that confronts the role player, rather than how he or she feels about it. Cases should be written in objective language which avoids judgmental statements and evaluative descriptions of behavior (stupid, thoughtless, lecherous, selfish, etc.). The case should state the problem or issue, but should not indicate how to deal with the case.

Focus

Roles should give the trainee an opportunity to focus on the training objective and should not be cluttered with irrelevant details. This means that case material which contains complicated technical processes must be avoided as the issues related to technical matters may entice the trainee away from the issue at hand.

The writer must be cautious about using material which is closely identified with well-known organizational problems and/or associated with particular individuals. Cases based on this type of material may embroil the trainees in the politics of that situation rather than the case at hand.

Conflict

Effective role plays require conflicting drives and motivations to propel the role players through the case and to sustain the interest of the observers. Types of conflict may range from minor issues to fairly important and major ones. Any type of conflict may be used as long as it seems realistic to the trainee group.

There are many sources of conflict. Some of the most common ones include: (1) conflicting motives and emotions, (2) conflicting roles, (3) perceptual differences, (4) divergent goals, (5) competition, (6) scarce resources, and (7) multiple sources of conflict.

Conflicting Motives and Emotions: This conflict relates to two or more incompatible drives in the same person, possibly resulting in depression, anger, or withdrawal. Example: The ambitious worker who is anxious about taking on more important tasks and greater responsibility. Example: The anti-authority employee who hates taking orders from a boss, but who badly needs a job.

Conflicting Roles: Everyone has a multitude of roles that they play in life. Sometimes this leads to role conflicts on the job. Example: The woman supervisor who is a successful mother, but who is tempted to treat her subordinates maternally rather than as employees.

Perceptual Differences: We see things through the light of our own experience and background. This can often cause two individuals to come to totally different conclusions about the same set of circumstances. Example: A vice-president of finance sees a production manager as effective and efficient because he or she has attempted to limit the number of products produced by the company. The vice-president of sales sees the production manager as an incompetent who is insensitive to the varied needs of his or her customers who have a need for a wide variety of products from the company.

Divergent Goals: Conflict can develop because of different goals between sub-units of the same organization or a difference between the goals of an employee and the organization. Example: Customer service may resent the manner in which the design engineering department designed a piece of machinery. The design makes it difficult to service. Design engineering created their design in order to conform to stylistic marketing considerations. Example: An individual wants to schedule his or her vacation at the same time that he or she will be needed for a critical phase of an important project.

Competition: Two or more persons may strive against each other for position or advantage. Example: Two managers who are vying to become the head of an important project.

Scarce Resources: In an organization, individuals and departments almost always are obliged to compete for available resources in setting up budgets and projects. This is a frequent source of conflict between individuals in the same organization. Example: Two different department heads attempt to entice the same highly qualified engineers for their own individual projects.

Multiple Sources of Conflict: In most conflict situations, there is more than one source of conflict present. Example: A supervisor who wants to be seen as a "good guy" orders his or her unwilling employees to work overtime and thus comes in conflict with a union steward who is attempting to oppose the overtime order vigorously. In this case, several sources of conflict are present. The supervisor has conflicting emotions. He or she has a need to be liked by his or her employees; at the same time, he or she knows the organization expects the overtime production. There is also role conflict in this case, as the supervisor must play his or her role as an arm of management and the union steward must represent the workers. In addition, if the union contract is ambiguous about the right of the company to require overtime, a conflict involving perceptual (or interpretive) differences arises. In developing role-playing cases, however, it is important that the number of different conflicts be limited so that the training objectives may be brought into sharp focus and therefore become that much more achievable.

Developing Observer Guides

The purpose of an observer guide is to concentrate the attention of the group on issues that are relevant to the objectives of the role-playing session. The post-enactment discussion is primarily based on the data from observer guides when they are utilized. It is clear that if an observer guide is going to be used, it must be structured and written in a way to facilitate communication about relevant issues, as well as to focus in on those issues.

There are two types of questions used in observer guides: (1) those concerned with content, and (2) those concerned with process.

Content questions are those which ask 'what happened?'– i.e.,:

(a) did he follow step 1?

(b) did she bring up the blocked issue?

(c) what decision was made?

(d) who brought up the thought about the painting?

Process questions attempt to get at communication, psychological, and motivational issues–i.e.,:

(a) how did Mary handle John's defensiveness?

(b) did Ben appear to be empathic? How?

Both content and process issues are relevant in all situations. Usually, observer guides contain both types of questions, since there are at least two or three objectives to be achieved. Remember to ask questions that are usable in a post-enactment discussion. If you do not want to discuss one person's role-playing effort, do not ask a question that would lead people to concentrate on an individual's effort. Rather, consider a broader question, such as, "How might you have handled the defensiveness of the employee?" Again, the objectives of the session should dictate the questions.

The samples shown in Figures 2 and 3 and those cited in Chapter III illustrate typical observer guides.

Figure 2

Sample Observer Guide

1. **Listening**

   A. Who did most of the talking in the early stages of the interview (the first ten minutes)?

   B. Who did most of the talking in the second phase of the interview (the second ten minutes)?

   C. Did the supervisor encourage the employee to air his or her views? Did the supervisor seem to be seeking honestly the employee's opinion or was he or she merely trying to refute the employee's arguments?

   D. Record each time the supervisor gives a counter-argument to the employee before the employee has fully explained his or her point of view.

   E. Note each time the supervisor gives a counter-argument to the employee before the employee has fully explained his or her point of view.

   F. How often does the interviewer give an understanding listening response? How often does he or she put the employee on the defensive? Give examples.

2. **Analyze and Weigh Facts**

   A. Do the supervisor and subordinate agree on what the problem is?

   (Note: During the early phases of the interview, the supervisor should try to get a clear and mutually agreed-upon statement of the problem before he or she presents counter-arguments or offers solutions.)

   Write down the statement of the problem as agreed upon between supervisor and subordinate.

Figure 2 (Continued)

(Note: Before attempting to solve the problem, the supervisor and subordinate should agree upon the basic facts.)

B. The supervisor should consider alternative solutions. What were some of the alternatives in the case? Were other possibilities overlooked? If so, why?

Figure 3

Sample Observer Guide

1. How clear and concise was the supervisor in presenting his or her idea?

2. Did the supervisor maintain good eye contact with the manager?

3. Did the supervisor clarify the issue by responding adequately to questions?

4. Did the manager seem to respond well to the proposal of the supervisor? How do you know?

5. Did you feel that each person was really listening?

6. How did the situation end? Would you have ended it differently? How?

VI.

RESOURCES

Any extensive bibliography on role playing is likely to include a broad range of subjects related to role playing, with references to other uses of role playing besides training—i.e., uses of role playing related to attitude change experiments, testing and diagnostic procedures, as well as its use in personnel assessment.

The references given below relate to role playing and its use only in the area of training. They refer broadly to those items which deal with some elements of the operational description and design format as illustrated in this book.

BIBLIOGRAPHY

Corsini, R., M. Shaw, and R. Blake. *Role Playing in Business and Industry.* New York: The Free Press of Glencoe, Inc., 1961.

Kellog, E.E. A Role-Playing Case: How to Get the Most Out of It. *Personnel Journal,* October 1954, *33,* 179-183.

Koppel, D.D. Sequential Role Playing. *Training,* July 1978, *15,* 43-44.

Maier, N.R.F. *Psychology in Industrial Organization,* 4th edition. Boston: Houghton Mifflin Company, 1973.

Maier, N.R.F. *et al. The Role-Play Technique.* La Jolla, California: University Associates, 1975.

Parry, S. *Using Role Playing in the Classroom.* New York: Training House, Inc., 1973.

Phelan, J.G. The Principles of Role-Playing. *Journal of the American Society of Training Directors,* December 1958, *12,* 3-13.

Shaw, M.E. Role-Playing. In R.L. Craig and L.R. Bittel (Eds.), *Training and Development Handbook.* New York: McGraw-Hill Book Company, 1967, 206-224.

Weiner, H.B., and J.S. Sacks. Warm-up and Sum-up Techniques. *Group Psychotherapy,* 1969, *22,* 1-14.

Wohlking, W. Guide to Writing Role-Playing Cases. *Training and Development Journal,* November 1966, 2-6.

Wohlking, W. Role Playing. In R.L. Craig (Ed.), *Training and Development Handbook,* Second Edition. New York: McGraw-Hill Book Company, 1976, 36-1 to 36-24.

Wohlking, W., and H.B. Weiner. Structured and Spontaneous Role Playing: Contrast and Comparison. *Training and Development Journal,* January 1971, 8-14.

WORKSHOPS

As this is written, there are no regularly scheduled, publicly available workshops on the role-playing approaches described in this book. However, the three organizations listed below all, from time to time, conduct workshops on role playing. The first one listed, Cornell University, includes in its workshops training in both method-centered role playing and developmental role playing. The other two organizations, MOHR Development, Inc., and Development Dimensions International, Inc., conduct workshops only on a specialized type of method-centered role playing known as behavior modeling. Workshops are also provided by the authors on an in-house basis. Further information about workshops can be obtained by writing these organizations:

1. New York State School of Industrial and Labor Relations, Cornell University, 3 East 43rd Street, New York, New York 10017.

2. MOHR Development, Inc., 1700 Bedford Street, Stamford, Connecticut 06905.

3. Development Dimensions International, Inc., 250 Mt. Lebanon Blvd. Suite 303, Pittsburg, Pennsylvania 15234.

APPENDIX

1. A Method-Centered Single Role Play:
   An Initial Sales Presentation

2. A Method-Centered Role Rotational Role Play:
   Conducting a Disciplinary Interview

3. A Method-Centered Multiple Role Play:
   Handling an Employee with a Discrimination Complaint

4. A Developmental Single Role Play:
   Dealing with an Unknown Problem

5. A Developmental Role Rotational Role Play:
   Handling a Complaining Customer

6. A Developmental Multiple Role Play:
   Handling an Employee's Pay Check Complaint

VII.

APPENDIX 1

A Method-Centered Single Role Play:
An Initial Sales Presentation

Objectives: The objectives of this session are to:
(1) give the trainees (managers, supervisors) a set of steps that can be used to handle effectively an initial sales presentation; and
(2) give the trainees an opportunity to see and analyze an actual sales presentation using the guidelines taught.

1. The Warm-Up

This is a two-part warm-up. It is designed to relax the trainees, raise their awareness about the issue at hand, and motivate them to learn and use the key steps.

A. On a chalkboard or flip chart, print the words SELLER and BUYER. Ask the group to develop a list for each. This list should be of the problems that each group faces in an initial sales presentation. Here are some thoughts on what the group may come up with . . .

Seller Problems

buyer doesn't listen

Buyer Problems

salesperson too pushy

75

buyer doesn't give enough time	salesperson is uninformed
buyer is really not interested and is wasting salesperson's time	salesperson talks too much and too quickly—not allowing enough time for questions
so much too say—hard to organize oneself and say everything in order	item not suitable to needs—or at least the salesperson does not relate item to needs of buyer
tired of going over the same points—buyer asks same questions over and over	not enough time—problem in getting relevant information quickly . . . etc.
buyer asks a question that seller doesn't know the answer to . . . etc.	

B. Once the group has exhausted problem areas, they should be ready to accept a set of guidelines to handle an initial sales call effectively. Go over these steps carefully and discuss them with the group so that everyone is clear about their use. (These guidelines should be put on the chalkboard and/or distributed.)

Guidelines for Handling an Initial Sales Presentation Effectively

1. Greet the buyer in a warm, friendly manner, introducing yourself by name.
2. Ask the person a question related to your product or service that will gain his or her attention. This question should relate directly to his or her needs.
3. Ask the person to describe his or her situation and needs in relation to your product/service area.
4. Explain how your product/service matches the needs expressed. Stress benefits of using product/service.
5. Explore any objections the buyer may have. Respond to each objection carefully, each time stressing a benefit.
6. Begin to sum up the presentation by reviewing product/service benefits and stressing *features* of product/service that would be of particular value to the buyer.

7. Close politely and strongly by asking for an order, or scheduling another meeting, if that appears necessary.

The instructor should then lead a discussion designed to clarify any questions the group may have about the steps which have been placed in front of the group. Go over each item on the list in sequence. Ask if there are any questions on each item. If there is any person in the group who suggests he or she does not understand a step—give one or two illustrations.

2. The Enactment

Explain to the group that they will now have an opportunity to see the steps in action. Two people will come to the front of the class and one will be a potential buyer—the other, the salesperson. Using the guidelines just reviewed, the two people will demonstrate an actual sales situation. While this is happening, the rest of the class will observe and respond to questions on the observer guides provided. These questions will then be reviewed in the post-enactment discussion.

Ask for volunteers to come up and demonstrate the steps. If no one volunteers, try to encourage several people to come up who have been maintaining strong eye contact with you and who have been outgoing and generally enthusiastic. Do not force volunteers. For more details, see Chapter III, The Warm-Up section, Selecting Role Players.

At this point, give the two role players their briefing sheets and distribute observer guides to the rest of the group.

Set the scene by saying something like:

"Our two volunteers are about to demonstrate how an actual sales presentation might happen. The salesperson is trying to sell the person on the use of his or her services as an (insurance person, stockbroker, ad executive, etc., leave it up to volunteers to choose an area they are comfortable with).

Let's see what happens when (*fill in name of volunteer*) tries to sell (*fill in name of volunteer*). Please use your observer guide . . .

"Let's begin . . ."

An Initial Sales Presentation: Role A

Role of Chris Brown, Salesperson

You have been an (insurance person, stockbroker, ad executive, real estate broker—choose one) for only six months. You love it so far. You have learned quickly and know that the firm you work for—Jones and Amber, Inc.—has been in business for 40 years and has one of the best reputations in the field. This firm has every resource possible. This means that you can give your customers the best advice on how to spend their money and get the most value. You have no doubt that anyone who comes on as a customer will save time and money. You have just met someone whom you feel is a good potential customer for the services of Jones and Amber. You have arranged a meeting and hope to convince him or her in one sitting to switch from the firm he or she is presently using. You feel the benefits are clear—lots of experience, a good research department, a good service department, and convenient location. You feel that once the needs of the client are defined, a list of what can and should be done can be developed.

An Initial Sales Presentation: Role B

Role of Pat Barrett, Buyer

You have been using your neighbor, Gene Smith, as your (insurance agent, stockbroker, ad executive, real estate broker—your fellow co-role player will let you know which) for five years. Gene is competent and you never really thought about changing. You do a substantial amount of business with this person. Gene works with a small firm. You never considered that as part of your reason for using Gene—it was simply a personal thing. A person from Jones and Amber, a much larger firm in the same line of work, has just called you to get together.

An Initial Sales Presentation: Observer Guide

This is a two-part observer guide. Answer both parts carefully.

I. For each of the steps below, note if the salesperson did or did not achieve it.

Step	*Yes*	*Somewhat*	*No*	*Unsure*
1. Greet the buyer in a warm, friendly manner, introducing himself or herself by name.				
2. Ask the buyer a question, related to the product or service that will gain his or her attention. This question should relate directly to his or her needs.				
3. Ask the person to describe the situation and needs in relation to the product/service area.				
4. Explain how the product/service matches the needs expressed. Stress benefits of using product/service.				
5. Explore any objections the buyer may have. Respond to each carefully, each time stressing a benefit.				
6. Begin to sum up the presentation by reviewing product/service benefits and stressing *features* of product/service that would be of particular value to the buyer.				
7. Close politely and strongly by asking for an order, or scheduling another meeting, if that appears necessary.				

II.

Would you say that this presentation was a success for the buyer? For the seller? Why and why not?

What things did the seller do that you felt were most effective?

What things did the seller do that you felt were not effective or that you might have done differently?

Were the problems noted in the warm-up part of this session handled by the demonstration? Which problems still existed for the buyer? For the seller?

3. The Post-Enactment Discussion

The purpose of the discussion is to reinforce the steps and get the trainees to see the value in using them in their own sales presentations.

While the enactment was happening in front of the group, the trainer should have been preparing large sheets of blank paper, each with a single question from the observer guide. Ideally, this would have been done prior to the session. At this point, when the enactment is completed, the group should jointly discuss the observer guide. In every case, the actual people who did the enactment should speak first, giving their assessment of their own performance. After they have commented, the others in the room can freely comment on their performances. *Emphasis should be placed on the steps which were used, not on steps omitted.*

VIII.

APPENDIX 2

A Method-Centered Role Rotational Role Play:
Conducting a Disciplinary Interview

Objective: The objective of this session is to teach the content and steps of a disciplinary interview.

1. The Warm-Up

The warm-up is designed to get participants thinking about the disciplinary process and to develop an awareness as to why interviews are not conducted, or if they are conducted, not conducted very well. The warm-up will also offer specific guidelines as to how to engage in an effective disciplinary interview.

The trainer should make comments along the following lines:

"Though all of you have heard of the disciplinary interview, many of you may not ever have conducted such an interview. If you do conduct them, perhaps you are not satisfied with what you do. Today we are discussing the role of this interview in the disciplinary process.

"First I would like to discuss with you some of the reasons why it is not conducted. Then I would like to talk about a set of guidelines for conducting that interview. A set of guidelines that can be used in a practice exercise."

The trainer should then make a statement such as:

"We know that many supervisors do not conduct disciplinary interviews or at least try to avoid conducting this type of interview. What do you think are the causes of this resistance?"

Participant answers should be listed on the chalkboard. The instructor *should not add anything unless he or she is sure the group has exhausted its ideas on the subject.* He or she should place at the top of the chalkboard or on a flip chart the phrase, "Reasons Why the Disciplinary Interview Is Not Conducted."

Below are some of the typical reasons supervisors will give for not conducting disciplinary interviews. The points which would be placed on the chalkboard are *italicized*. The words that follow are elaborations on the thoughts that need not be placed on the board or flip chart.

- *The Role of Villain*: Few people like to be villains.

- *Lack of Skill*: Some supervisors don't know how to conduct the interview.

- *Hostility Instead of Discipline*: Some supervisors think the employee has been sufficiently warned or punished, if the supervisor is hostile or cold and aloof with the employee at the time of the rule violation.

- *Discomfort with Confrontation*: Most supervisors don't like confrontation: It makes them nervous and uncomfortable.

- *Loss of Friendship*: The interview may seem damaging to a friendship.

- *Time Loss*: The interview takes valuable time.

- *Lose Temper*: The supervisor is afraid he or she may lose his or her temper once he or she starts speaking about the rule violation.

- *Rationalization*: The employee knows he or she did the wrong thing, so "why should I talk to him or her about it?"

- *"The Only One"*: Nobody else may be conducting discipline interviews, so "why should I?"

- *Guilt*: The feeling "how can I discipline someone if I have done the same thing?"

- *Fear*: Fear the management won't back you up.

After comments from the group have been placed on the board, the instructor may supply some of the points—not necessarily *all*—that were mentioned by the group.

The trainer should then point out that one of the reasons for not conducting the interview is that supervisors do not know how to conduct it. The trainer should now tell the group that a correctly conducted disciplinary interview is possible, if certain steps are followed. He or she should then state that the exercise which follows will deal with this problem. He or she should then produce the key steps to follow and post them in front of the class or write them on the board. It should be as follows:

Guidelines in Conducting a Disciplinary Interview

1. State the problem.

2. Ask employee for his or her point of view about the problem.

3. Inform employee of your expectations for improvement.

4. Tell the employee of consequences if there is insufficient improvement.

5. If necessary, set up a follow-up meeting.

The instructor should then lead a discussion designed to clarify any questions the group may have about the steps which have been placed in front of the group. Go over each item on the list in sequence. Ask if there are any questions on each item. If there is any person in the group who suggests he or she does not understand a step, give one or two illustrations.

2. The Enactment

Tell the group that there will now be an exercise on the use of the procedure in handling a disciplinary interview. Inform participants that the case you are about to present has two roles: (1) the supervisor's role and (2) the employee's role.

Then, ask for a volunteer to play the employee's role. Wait at least 20 seconds before you give up on getting a volunteer. Count to 20 slowly, if necessary. In almost all cases, someone will volunteer for the role. If this procedure does not work, choose someone who retains eye contact with you. If no one does this, pick somebody from the group. The standards for selection should be:

(1) eye contact;

(2) someone who does not appear to be overly anxious;

(3) someone who has, in your opinion, been articulate in the discussions that have taken place thus far in class; and

(4) if more than one person is available, choose the person who is most animated and verbal.

After you have obtained a person from the class to play the role of the employee, ask him or her to leave the room for a moment. Tell him or her to station himself or herself immediately outside of the classroom door and say that you will be with him or her in just a moment. Before he or she leaves, give him or her the employee's role (Role B). Tell him or her to read the role and say you will check with him or her shortly to see if he or she has any questions about the role. After he or she has left the room, you will then work with the group.

Distribute copies of the supervisor's role (Role A) to everyone in the class. Tell them to read the role and be prepared to conduct the disciplinary interview with the employee who will soon come into the room. State that you will conduct about three to four role plays with different supervisors; then ask if anyone has any questions about the content of the supervisor's role.

Ask for a volunteer to play the role of the supervisor. If there are no volunteers, use the same procedures described above for getting a person to role play the employee's role. Then, have that person come up to the front of the room where you have set up two chairs facing each other.

While the class has been reading the supervisor's role, you should step out briefly and see if the employee has any questions about his or her role. Also, give him or her the following instructions:

> Play your role as naturally as possible. If you feel the supervisor is allowing you to talk and explain your position, attempt to elaborate on how you feel about the problem. If you feel the supervisor is not really listening to you or is somewhat hostile, you may want to respond to that by being somewhat uncommunicative yourself or hostile.

If the role player asks you any questions about the facts of the case, simply restate them as best you understand them. Tell him or her that he or she may make up any facts which are necessary to make the interview coherent, but in no way should such new facts create a distortion in the role-playing situation.

Start the role play. After the "supervisor" has been seated, ask the "employee" outside to come into the room and sit down opposite the manager. Then, make the following statement:

> You, the employee, have just knocked on the supervisor's door and you have been invited to come in. The supervisor starts the interview.

Step back away from the scene of action and sit down in a chair, making yourself relatively inconspicuous. You may want to take notes on what transpires. If you do this, do not be obvious about it, since note-taking by the instructor sometimes disturbs role players. When listening to the interview, make mental notes on how well the *procedure* is followed.

After the interview is completed, make the following statement to the group:

> We have just seen how one supervisor handles his or her disciplinary interview. May we have another volunteer to conduct a similar interview using his or her own particular style and approach?

If you do not get a volunteer, use the same procedures recommended in the Enactment section of this Appendix.

Allow three to four plays of this nature to take place. In this case, do not allow any role play to exceed ten minutes. If the ten-minute limit is exceeded or if the interview is becoming repetitive, cut off the role play and get another volunteer to play the supervisor.

The Phone-In Case: Role A

Role of Tracy Fenton, Supervisor

You are Tracy Fenton, a department supervisor. Yesterday, one of your employees, Terry Miller, did not come to work and did not call in. This also happened several months ago. Terry has been with you six months and is past his probationary period.

Terry Miller was out sick once before. At that time, Terry failed to phone in to inform you that he would be out. You talked to Terry about it the following day. You were low-key in your approach. You don't like to upset your employees, if it is not necessary.

Because this is the second time Terry did not call in, you have asked that Terry see you after the coffee break. You feel that calling in is important because it permits you to better organize and piece out work in your department. Also, a failure to call in is a violation of the organization's work rules.

You have just greeted Terry Miller, who has seated himself alongside your desk.

The Phone-In Case: Role B

Role of Terry Miller, Employee

You are Terry Miller, an employee and your supervisor is Tracy Fenton. You have been working here for six months and have completed your trial period. You did not come in yesterday. You were sick with a headache and cramps. You think it was a short-term virus.

You were out with a similar condition earlier this year. At that time, Tracy Fenton informed you that you should call in early whenever you expect to be absent. As it was said informally, you thought that calling in is probably "no big deal," even though you *do* have a phone. Also, you were very sick. Furthermore, in your last job, whenever you did call in, your supervisor hassled you. Therefore, calling in is something you prefer not to do.

This morning, your supervisor requested that you see him following the morning break. As the scene opens, you have just said "hello" to your boss, Tracy Fenton. You have just sat opposite Tracy at his desk.

Remember . . . .
- You think that there may possibly be some questions about your absence—but you were *really* sick.
- You react to your boss based on the manner he related to you. If Tracy Fenton is reasonable . . . you are reasonable. If Tracy comes on aggressive . . . you react in kind.
- You do have other people at home besides yourself.

3. The Post-Enactment Discussion

The basic purposes of this post-enactment discussion are two-fold: (1) to reinforce the correct use of the procedures discussed in the warm-up—the content dimension of the role play, and (2) to discuss criteria for *how* the interview should be conducted—the process dimension of the role play.

In general, the content of the interview has to do with the substance of the supervisor's conversation, e.g., the procedures which were followed. The "how" part of the interview has to do with the manner in which the supervisor conducted the interview, e.g., his attitude toward the subordinate, his communication techniques, or his personal style.

At the conclusion of the role play, the trainer should stand beside the flip chart or chalkboard which has the five points that should have been covered in the disciplinary interview (as below).

- State the problem.

- Ask employee for his or her point of view about the problem.

- Inform employee of your expectations for improvement.

- Tell the employee of consequences if there is insufficient improvement.

- If necessary, set up a follow-up meeting.

Then, inform the class that you would like to go down the checklist to determine which points were covered. In general, most supervisors will cover the first three points well and often be weak on the last two points. As you go down each individual point, questions will arise regarding the discipline procedure. This will give you an opportunity to fully clarify points about the disciplinary interview.

In general, the trainer should try to have the class avoid mentioning the names of particular role players. The focus of the discussion should be on the steps in the discipline interview and not who did what. The instructor should then point to the steps which everyone seems to include. There should be positive reinforcement regarding the steps which were followed.

Participants will normally raise points about the manner and style with which the interview was conducted. Explain that first the substantive points will be covered and then style and manner will be discussed.

After the various steps have been discussed, pose the following discussion question to the class:

> What, in your opinion, were the things done that caused the interview to go well in terms of style?

As the participants give their comments, they should be listed on the chalkboard. Comments about style and content may be often mixed in one statement. Classify each comment according to the chart on the chalkboard. In general, comments having to do with attitudes and communication techniques should be classified under "style." The following types of responses should be listed in the "appropriate styles" column.

Examples of *appropriate styles* might include:

- listen carefully;

- be calm;

- attempt to make employee comfortable;

- focus on the problem rather than person;

- maintain the employee's self-esteem; and

- come to the point.

Then, the trainer should ask the question, "In general, without reference to the role playing you have seen, but just based on your own experience, what styles are inappropriate?," listing class comments on the chalkboard.

Examples of *inappropriate styles* might include:

- anger;

- interrupting;

- apologetic tone;

- putting the employee down; and

- rambling away from the topic.

The group may not raise all of the points indicated in the above lists. Suggest any items which were not brought up by participants after the group has had a reasonable opportunity to comment.

In any time that remains, ask the group how they feel these concepts can be applied to their on-the-job situations. If they have problems trying to apply the concepts in the lesson, redirect the question to the group. In other words, do not try to answer all the questions yourself. Let some of the group members interpret to the rest of the group how the concepts in the lesson should be applied. If the group does not respond to the "redirected question," only then comment on the question yourself.

IX.

APPENDIX 3

A Method-Centered Multiple Role Play:
Handling an Employee with a Discrimination Complaint

Objectives: The objectives of this session are to:
  (1) give the trainees (managers, supervisors) a set of steps that can be used to effectively handle a discrimination complaint; and
  (2) give these trainees an opportunity to practice the skill of handling this type of interview.

1. The Warm-Up

This is a three-part warm-up. It is designed to relax the trainees, raise their awareness about the issue at hand, and motivate them to learn and use the key steps.

1. On a chalkboard or flip chart at the front of the room, print in large block letters the terms:

MALE FEMALE BLACK HISPANIC WHITE YOUNG OLD

For each term, start a new section on the board or piece of paper. For each term, have the trainees list stereotype words associated with each. Allow people to just call out while you write the stereotype terms under the heading. Try to get at least 15 or so terms under each heading. These charts can then be taped up around the room during the remainder of the session. They serve to remind people that these stereotypes can often serve to prevent honest, effective dealing with a discrimination complaint.

2. Now that the group has an idea that prejudice has an impact on the topic, move into the more direct link with the job situation. Ask the group to list problems they would have, or they could foresee others having, handling a person making a complaint of discrimination. The list will probably look something like this:

Problems Dealing with Complaints
(from viewpoint of manager/supervisor)

1. Complainer is hostile.

2. I don't understand what the problem is.

3. I get upset and nervous.

4. Complainer says I'm unfair and unsympathetic.

5. I'm not sure if I should agree, disagree, or be neutral in the situation.

6. My own attitudes don't go along with this idea of complaining. We never had those privileges in the "old days."

7. Worried that more complaints will follow if I "give in."

8. Don't know if I should defend the organization or not.

Now it might be a good idea to ask the trainees if they were the ones making the discrimination complaint, what might be their concerns?

Concerns of Complainer

1. Fear I'd get fired.

2. Fear I'd be thought a troublemaker or disloyal.

3. Fear my colleagues would ostracize me.

4. Fear people would laugh at my complaint.

5. Figure they wouldn't really do anything about it and being sorry I brought it up.

Developing both these lists should have trainees aware and concerned about the complexity of the problem. They should now be ready to go over the steps for the effective interview. Read the steps carefully to the group. Have them printed on a flip chart or on the chalkboard. The trainer may also wish to have the steps reproduced and distributed to the group.

3. In this last part of the warm-up, carefully go through the key steps. These steps should be followed by every trainee role playing the supervisor during the enactment stage of the session.

Guidelines for Handling a Discrimination Complaint

1. Ask the employee to state the situation carefully.

2. Listen attentively to the employee to understand both the information being stated and the person's feelings about the situation.

3. Repeat or rephrase the statements of the employee to make certain you have a clear understanding of the situation from his or her perspective.

4. Tell the employee that you will thoroughly investigate the situation and bring the complaint to the attention of Personnel.

5. Arrange a meeting with the employee during the interview within two weeks to discuss the results of the investigation.

6. Close the meeting in a positive way.

The instructor should then lead a discussion designed to clarify any questions the group may have about the steps which have been placed in front of them. Go over each item on the list in sequence. Ask if there are any questions on each item. If there is any person in the group who suggests he or she does not understand a step, give one or two illustrations.

2. The Enactment

Break up the class into groups of three. One person in the group will role play the part of the supervisor, one will role play the part of the employee, and the third will serve as an observer, using the observer guide provided. Each person should be given the briefing sheet to use for his or her part of the observer guide.

Then, the trainer sets the scene by explaining the basic situation:

> You are now going to be in a situation involving a discrimination complaint. One of you will be the super-visor—Dale. The person playing this part should try to follow the key steps we just reviewed in the warm-up. One of you will be role playing the part of Jan, an employee who feels discriminated against because he or she was passed over for promotion. The promotion was given to the other person just because he or she was a minority person. The third person in the group will observe the role play and attempt to respond to questions on the observer guide. When the role plays are completed, we will come together again and discuss what happened.

Begin . . . .

The Job Promotion Case: Role A

Role of Dale Evers, Supervisor
You have been a supervisor in this department for ten years. The group has 20 people split fairly evenly between men and women (12

men, eight women). There are three black men and four black women. Also, there is an Hispanic male. You feel this is a good mix and everyone gets along very well. When you came ten years ago, the department was all-white-male. You feel the changes are definitely for the better. You are behind the company efforts 100 percent to give everyone a fair break. Recently, a promotion came up and you gave it to the most eligible person—who happened to be a black male. There was no doubt in your mind he was the best qualified to handle the increased responsibility. The job involved a tremendous amount of travel and this person—Bob—had often mentioned that he wanted to travel. You realize that perhaps two or three other people might have done well with the job, but they did not have the experience Bob did. You are worried that Jan Brown wants to see you about this issue. Jan has stated several times that he or she deserves a promotion—and you agree. You think that Jan might contend he or she would have been better suited than Bob for the recent promotion.

As the scene opens, Jan has just greeted you and seated himself or herself opposite you.

The Job Promotion Case: Role B

Role of Jan Brown, Employee

You have been in the department five years. You like working for Dale Evers, whom you feel is both talented and fair. There are 20 people in the department—12 men and eight women. There are three black men and four black women—and one of the men is Hispanic. You like the group and have lots of friends—people you not only enjoy working with but also seeing after work. You feel you are not prejudiced. Recently, a promotion came up and Bob, one of the black guys in the group, got it. You feel that although Bob is an OK guy, he isn't as bright as you—and certainly no better for the spot than you. The job involves a good deal of travel. Bob's married, with kids, and you are single. You feel that makes it better for you than for him. Also, you sense that Bob's being black was more the reason than anything else why he was chosen. You have gotten good performance reviews. You think you recall that Bob complained about his reviews last year, so you probably have better evaluations. You agree that minorities deserve a break, but this is clearly unfair. You are going to tell Dale how you feel.

As the scene opens, you just greeted Dale and sat yourself opposite him or her.

The Job Promotion Case: Observer Guide

During the role play, try to answer the following questions:

I. Did the supervisor:

Yes   Somewhat   No   Unsure

Ask the employee to state the situation carefully?

Listen attentively to the employee to understand the information being stated and the person's feelings about the situation?

Repeat or rephrase the statements of the employee to make certain he or she had a clear understanding of the situation?

Tell the employee that the complaint will be investigated and brought to the attention of Personnel?

Arrange a meeting with the employee to discuss the results of the investigation?

Close the meeting in a positive way?

II. Other Questions

Did the supervisor appear genuinely interested and concerned? If yes, what behaviors made you feel that way? If not, why not?

Do you feel that the employee was satisfied with the results of the interview? Why or why not?

If you had been the supervisor, what might you have done—
   (1) in the same way?
   (2) differently?

Why?

3. The Post-Enactment Discussion

When each triad has completed the role play, bring the group together. While the group was role playing, the observer guide questions should have been put on the chalkboard or on flip charts. At this time, go through each question separately and get answers to each of the guide questions. This information can then be used to discuss the issues that are still problems for the group and reinforce the areas where the group is successful.

The final part of the discussion could be to go back to the lists of problem areas for the supervisor and the employee that were developed during the warm-up. Allow the group to comment on how they now feel about overcoming each of these problems.

X.

APPENDIX 4

A Developmental Single Role Play:
Dealing with an Unknown Problem

Objective: This session is designed to assist managers in improving their skills in interpersonal communications.

1. The Warm-Up

This warm-up has two parts. First, ask the group to define the term 'hidden agenda.' List everyone's ideas on a flip chart or chalkboard. Have the group come to a common understanding of the term to mean a problem not openly discussed.

Second, ask the group to list ways this type of problem should be dealt with. The list might include some of the following thoughts:

- attempt to create a climate of trust;

- listen without interrupting;

- try not to make evaluative or judgmental statements;

- demonstrate understanding by nodding the head and the use of the phrase "uh-huh" at appropriate points, summarize the conversation;

- repeat phrases made by the person to demonstrate you understand the problem;

- try not to offer advice to the person but help him or her surface the problem;

- maintain appropriate eye contact with interviewee; and

- avoid negative body language, i.e., don't cross arms.

Do not force the group to come up with these ideas. The point is to let the group list their ideas and try the role play.

2. The Enactment

Using the guidelines in Chapter III, The Warm-Up section, Selecting Role Players, choose people for the roles of Lee Barker, Assistant Department Head, and Henry Barrett, Department Head. Give these individuals a chance to study their briefing sheets before coming up to the front of the group and beginning the role play. The rest of the group will be observing the enactment. Set the scene by saying something like:

> We are about to see how (*name of volunteer*) handles the unknown problem of his or her employee. That part will be played by (*name of volunteer*). Observe how this manager tries to "solve" the situation. O.K., let's get started . . .

The Lee Barker–Henry Barrett Case: Role A

Role of Henry Barrett, Department Head
You have been with the company about eight years and you are satisfied that you are doing an effective job. In general, you feel that the morale and efficiency of your department are high. You have two good people who, in your opinion, keep your department running—Lee Barker, your Assistant Department Head, and his new assistant, Ted West. Lee Barker has been in your department since he or she came to the company. After two years, you were sufficiently impressed with him or her to make him or her your assistant, promoting him or her over those who had much greater seniority.

Recently, however, a problem has developed. Lee, who, in your opinion, is the best person in your department, has been slipping somewhat. Twice in the last month reports have been turned in late. This has been of some concern to you, since these reports have affected your relationships with other departments. The last time this happened was a few days ago. You are quite concerned that this situation does not continue. Therefore, this morning you asked Lee to drop around for a chat sometime during the day.

As the scene opens, Lee has just been seated in your office, and you start to speak.

The Lee Barker–Henry Barrett Case: Role B

Role of Lee Barker, Assistant Department Head

You came into the organization about five years ago straight from college. Through a series of circumstances early in the job, you became closely attached to your department head, Henry Barrett. After the completion of your second year in the department, you were made assistant to him. Your advance has been regarded as extremely rapid, since you are relatively young and skipped over several others with much greater seniority in the department. Until about six months ago, you were quite pleased with the situation and felt that your future with the company was quite bright. However, another personality has entered into the field—Ted West. West entered the organization about three years ago and recently was made your assistant. He does a good job; however, he still has a lot to learn about the company, and, in particular, your department.

The promotional picture throughout the corporation during the time you have been with the company has been a very active one, and you feel that it is possible in the near future that your own boss may be promoted and his job may be open. What disturbs you is that a rumor has been going around that Ted West is now in his favor more than you are and has been given tasks of increasing responsibility. He has almost as frequent access to the department head, your boss, as you do.

Meanwhile, your boss, Henry Barrett, has done nothing to inform you about the situation one way or another about where you stand. As a result, you feel that your morale has been slipping. One of the by-products of the situation has been that twice in a month you have been late in getting your reports in to the department head. You are hopeful that your boss will take the initiative and try to clear up the situation in the near future. You are, of course, somewhat reluctant to raise the issue with him.

This morning he asked you to drop around and see him some time today. As the scene opens, you have just seated yourself in his office, and he starts to speak.

3. The Post-Enactment Discussion

After role play, ask the person role playing the department head if he or she felt he or she had uncovered and dealt with the real problem.

Next, ask the person role playing Lee to comment on that response.

Ask the group to comment on those communications techniques that appeared to be the most helpful. List these on a flip chart or chalkboard. Have the group add to the list other techniques that might have been helpful.

Attempt to develop some generalizations about effective and poor communications from this discussion, placing them on the chalkboard. Avoid having the person who role played Henry Barrett become the target of criticism.

XI.

APPENDIX 5

A Developmental Role Rotational Role Play:
Handling a Complaining Customer

Objectives: The objectives of this session are to:
- (1) give trainees an opportunity to develop and experiment with concepts and strategies for dealing with a complaining customer; and
- (2) give trainees an opportunity to practice their skills in handling a complaining customer.

1. The Warm-Up

The trainer opens the class by stating in his or her own words the following idea: For those who are in the retail business, handling customer complaints is a situation one deals with on a regular basis. It is one of the less attractive elements in a retail person's work life. Handling these problems takes tact and diplomacy, even though some complaints are irrational.

The trainer then says, "Some or all of you in the group have had experience with customer complaints. What are some of the more unusual complaints you have had to deal with?"

As participants give examples, list the examples on the chalkboard in abbreviated form.

After this list has been completed, inform the group that today you have an exercise that will require some of the participants to handle a customer complaint—and that you expect several people will do it.

Use the guidelines for selecting role players as suggested in Chapter III, The Warm-Up section, Selecting Role Players.

2. The Enactment

Set the scene by stating something like: "We are now going to see how several different people attempt to handle a customer who is upset by what is considered to be poor service. Our first role players (name them) are in place . . . Let's see how it goes. . . ."

The Case of the Complaining Customer: Role A

Role of Courtney King, Department Store Manager
You are the manager of the town's largest department store. You are seated at your desk, when someone who apparently is a customer has just entered your office.

The Case of the Complaining Customer: Role B

The Role of Sandy Mason, Customer
You have been shopping in your town's largest department store. You were looking at some clothing when a clerk came over to you and asked if he or she could offer any help. At that time, you declined. You browsed around some more, then decided on an item of clothing that you wanted.

At this time you went over to the same clerk who previously offered you some help but who was now involved in putting away some boxes. You said that you needed some help. The clerk then said, "Are you *sure* you want help now?" You feel that both words and tone were unjustified.

You have shopped in this store for over ten years and you have never received treatment like this. You decide that you are going to speak to the store manager. You are upset, and you feel that the clerk should be reprimanded.

As the scene opens, you have just walked into the manager's office.

3. **The Post-Enactment Discussion**

Place list of participants' suggestions on the chalkboard with title: "Approaches for Calming Complaining Customer."

1. Ask the group how they think a request to reprimand an employee under these circumstances should be handled.
2. Ask the participant playing the customer's role what kinds of things the manager said that he or she felt were responsive and led to his or her feeling better about the situation.
3. Ask the group what they liked about how this problem was handled in the role plays.
4. What kinds of things said by the various managers seemed to quiet and calm the customer down?

XII.

APPENDIX 6

A Developmental Multiple Role Play:
Handling an Employee's Pay Check Complaint

Objectives: The objectives of this session are to:
  (1) develop analytical ability in making decisions about an employee's complaint; and
  (2) develop skill in responding to an employee's complaint.

1. The Warm-Up

The instructor should tell the class that the session will focus on handling an employee's complaint. The session will deal with (1) the criteria to be considered in making a decision about the complaint, and (2) the manner with which the employee should be dealt.

We are all familiar with difficult supervisory decisions which have to do with employee requests, which, if not granted, may lead to complaints.

  • *Example 1*: An employee has asked to leave regularly five minutes before the end of the work day because of a change in the bus schedule. His or her next possible bus leaves an hour later.

  • *Example 2*: An employee wants to play a radio at his or her

> job, which is a boring one. There are no employees
> normally in his or her vicinity, but there is a
> company rule that prohibits radio playing on the
> job.

The instructor should then ask the participants the
following question: "What kinds of reasons would you use
for turning down a request regarding an employee complaint?"

Eliciting suggestions from the group might produce some
of the elements below, which could be used to decide how to
respond to an employee complaint. Participant suggestions
should be placed on a flip chart or chalkboard. Suggestions
which might be elicited could include:

- If it looks like favoritism to other employees.

- If the expense is too great.

- It violates existing policies.

- It may set a precedent which could complicate orderly
  administration.

The above list is not inclusive. It is only meant to be
illustrative. After a list is developed, tell the participants they
will now have an opportunity to apply some of these ideas in
an actual situation.

2. The Enactment

The instructor states:

> The role-playing case which will now be distributed is
> designed to illustrate several basic factors in handling
> grievances. As this exercise will be conducted as a multiple
> role play, you will all have an opportunity to participate
> and learn from the experience. We will first enact the role
> play and then discuss it.

A. *Assign Roles.* Have each person in the room count off alternately in "A's" and "B's." If there is an odd number, make that odd person a floating observer of role plays.

B. *Pass Out Roles.* To each person who is an "A," give a copy of the Tracy Singer role (Role A). To each "B," give the role of Jerry Shaw (Role B).

C. *Instructions to Role Players.* Give the following instructions to the role players:

Tell the participants that they should read the briefing sheets carefully and be prepared to enter into a role play after they read them. State that they have approximately three to five minutes to read the role. State that if they have any questions, they should raise their hands and you will come over and clarify whatever is necessary. Instruct the participants not to exchange information concerning the roles with their partners.

If anyone asks if the employee is a union member, make your decision based on the status of the participants. If most of the participants have union employees under them, answer the question as, "Yes, the employee is a union member." If most of the participants do not have union employees under them, answer the question with a "no."

D. *Commence Role Play.* After you are satisfied that everyone has read his or her role, commence the role play. It is often helpful to have people get away from the table and away from other role plays so that they can physically look directly at each other, as might be the case during any realistic confrontation between an employee and a supervisor. Immediately before commencing the role play, make the following statement to the group:

> As you talk to your partner, please attempt to refrain from looking at your role-play briefing sheet. You may do so if necessary, but only if you are quite uncertain as to particular key facts in your role.

E. *Monitor Role Play.* Make sure that everybody is engaged

in some type of discussion. If people look hesitant or uncertain, ask them if they have any questions about the role play. The role play itself will, typically, take between eight and 12 minutes. Try to have everyone complete the role play. If all but a few have completed the role play after about ten or 12 minutes, make an announcement to the group as follows: "Participants should try and complete the role plays within the next two minutes."

Preparation for the Post-Enactment Discussion

While the class is engaged in the role play, draw the chart below on the chalkboard or flip chart. Do the chart toward the latter part of the discussion. This will reduce the possibility that role players will be influenced in their decision by seeing the chart.

TYPE OF DECISION	TALLY	TOTALS
DENIED		
GRANTED		
GO TO PLANT MANAGER		
OTHER		

You will use this to gather and classify the data produced by the interviewers. A further explanation follows under the Post-Enactment Discussion.

The Pay Check Problem: Role A

The Role of Tracy Singer, Department Head

You are head of a department. In December of last year, a new policy was created related to absences. The policy was put into effect at the beginning of the current year. Notice of it was posted on the bulletin board on January 4. The new policy contains the following wording:

> Employees will not be paid for absences in excess of ten days in any calendar year. Exception to this policy may be made with the approval of the Plant Manager.

Jerry Shaw, one of your employees, has worked for you for six years. Last year, he was absent for 18 days. Jerry was paid for all of his absences. Last week, on December 4, he called and said he would be unable to work on December 4 or 5.

When Jerry spoke to you, it was apparent that he was somewhat agitated. His wife's illness seemed to be the cause. As you spoke to him, you figured that it was not a good time to go over the absentee policy; nor find out why Jerry was planning to be out two days instead of one. He is a good worker; however, in your opinion he becomes rattled easily. Because of this, you preferred not to have a long conversation with him. Nor did you think it wise to ask him many questions, as he appeared to be so distracted by his wife's condition. You thought that he would prefer to remain at home for one more day. You felt he wanted to be sure that his family was being taken care of, even though it would cost him one day's pay. You feel that as he was paid 18 days last year for days not worked, he probably has a fairly good attitude about the organization. Furthermore, he probably is aware of the importance of having a policy that deals with excessive absenteeism.

Your records indicate that he had been absent nine days prior to December 4. Therefore, December 4 is the last day to which he is entitled to a paid absence. Under the current policy, Jerry will not be entitled to pay for December 5.

Jerry Shaw has just requested a meeting with you. As the scene opens, he has just come into your office.

The Pay Check Problem: Role B

The Role of Jerry Shaw, Employee

You have worked in the organization for the last six years. Last year you had a run of bad luck and were out for 18 days with illness. Because of the organization's absence policy, you were paid for all the days you were out.

Before December 4 of this year, you had been out with one thing or another for nine days. On December 4, your wife became quite ill. When this occurred, you tried to have a relative come over, but this turned out not to be possible. You have two young children who require someone at home all day. After considerable effort on your part, you were able to obtain the services of a paid housekeeper. However, she was unable to start work until December 6. On December 4, you telephoned the head of your department, Tracy Singer, and explained the situation. At that time, you stated that you could not return to work until December 6. Tracy simply said "OK," and that was the end of the conversation.

On December 13, you were given your pay check. You saw it was short one day's wages. You checked with the payroll department and they said that you were not paid for December 5. The payroll clerk said that this was based on the new policy having to do with absences.

You are very agitated about this. This is the first time you have ever heard of this policy. Furthermore, your supervisor, Tracy Singer, said nothing about this when you phoned him. Also, he said nothing about it when you returned to work. You are annoyed and upset. In previous years, you were reimbursed for all your lost time. Therefore, you are confused by the fact that this year they are not paying you for December 5. Your total days out this year is only 11. You have never received any personal notification of this new policy. You feel it isn't fair to lose wages without being told about it before it occurs. In your opinion, you had a good reason to be away from work; consequently, you think you deserve your one day's pay.

You requested a meeting with your supervisor, Tracy Singer. As the scene opens, you have just entered his office.

3. The Post-Enactment Discussion

The instructor first (a) explains the categories on the chalkboard or the flip chart; (b) records the data produced by each instructor; and (c) discusses the data and the interview.

A. Explanation of the Categories

The instructor explains that on the chalkboard, participants will see four possible interview outcomes. He or she explains the categories, indicating that the first category is "denied." This means that the supervisor denied the grievance and offers no further recourse.

The second category is "granted." This means the supervisor will grant the employee's request and take personal responsibility for this decision. The third category is "go to plant manager." This means the supervisor will take the employee's grievance to the plant manager—usually with a request that the day's pay be granted.

The last category is "other." With this type of decision, the supervisor usually makes some type of arrangement where a swap is involved. Some examples: The man will receive the pay, but he will have to work it off in overtime hours. There are other variations of this theme.

B. Data Roundup

The instructor then states: "Starting on my left, I am now going to ask each supervisor about the kind of decision made. After I get the decision, I will place a record of it on the chart. When we have completed the data roundup, I will tally the results."

As you go around the room, tally each decision onto the chart. Then total each decision. Many of the participants will attempt to give fairly elaborate rationales to justify their decisions. Tell them that the individual experiences will be discussed later and that for the present you just want to get a tally of overall results.

Below is an example of how a typical data roundup might look completed and entered on the chart (assuming 12 interviews):

TYPE OF DECISION	TALLY	TOTALS
DENIED	ЖН II	7
GRANTED	I	1
GO TO PLANT MANAGER	III	3
OTHER	I	1

After summarizing the results, you may want to allow some of the individual managers, who have been particularly eager to explain their positions, some time to talk. Try to limit this to five to seven minutes. If the discussion is allowed to go longer, it will create repetitiveness later in the session.

C. Discussion of Data

The discussion of the data is divided into two parts: (1) Part I is a discussion concerning the implications of various types of decisions which can emerge from the discussions between the supervisor and the employee; (2) Part II is designed to deal with the process dimensions of the case. In this section, there is a focus on the interpersonal relations approach used by the supervisor in handling the grievance. The Part II discussion is optional and may be omitted if time starts to run out.

Part I. Content: What Are the Implications of the Decision?

The instructor then asks the following question: "What are the implications of denying the request?"

Place the response on the chalkboard. Below are some acceptable responses in this category:

- It will frustrate the employee.

- A grievance may be filed (if there is a union).

- The supervisor will demonstrate his or her ability to handle a problem at his or her level of management.

The instructor then asks the following question: "What would be the consequences of granting the request?"

Place the responses on the chalkboard. Below are some acceptable consequences:

- The employee will feel increased loyalty toward the supervisor.

- The supervisor will get himself or herself in trouble with management for violating policy.

- The supervisor may set a precedent which may be expensive to the organization.

The instructor then poses the following discussion question: "What are the implications of going to the plant manager?"

Place the responses on the board. Below are some acceptable responses in this category:

- The employee will be pleased that you plan to take some action on his or her case.

- If the plant supervisor is "tough," he or she may think the supervisor is weak in passing this decision to him or her.

- You are following an acceptable procedure and carrying out the intentions of management by taking a case with extenuating circumstances to the plant manager.

- If one does go to the plant manager, it is better to go with recommendations for or against the employee request, or else the plant manager will feel the supervisor is not doing his or her job.

The instructor then poses the following discussion question: "What are the implications of the 'other' type solutions?"

Below are some typical comments which can be expected:

- Making a "deal" on overtime, vacation, or holidays may set an undesirable precedent.

- It may be an acceptable compromise, *if* the likelihood of precedent setting is remote.

Typically, the most frequently chosen categories are "denied" and "go to plant manager." Our experience, based on both business and non-profit organization training experiences, is that "denied" was the decision most frequently chosen.

"Denied" is an acceptable solution if one is willing to live with a somewhat frustrated worker (who may file a grievance). Going to the plant manager would seem to be the most reasonable solution. There are extenuating circumstances in the case, and the personnel policy seems explicitly designed to deal with the kind of problem which has arisen. The only time it would not be desirable, from the supervisor's point of view, is if the supervisor has a particularly "hard nosed" type plant manager. However, since the case does not provide clues about the personality of the plant manager, participants are likely to assume the manager to have a temperament similar to that of their own immediate supervisor and make their decisions accordingly.

Summarize the implications of each category. You may want to suggest that both "denied" and "go to plant manager" are about equally acceptable decisions in terms of sound managerial practice, but in actuality, one would have to know more about the context of the situation to know if one's decisions were the best for the situation.

Part II. Process: How the Interview Was Handled

You have now reviewed with the group key elements having to do with the quality of decision. Now, discussion will focus on the manner in which the case was handled. Basically, you will discuss those factors under the control of the supervisor which are (1) desirable in creating effective communication between the supervisor and the employee, and (2) undesirable in communicating with the employee.

The instructor then poses the following discussion questions:

- "How many of you who played the role of employee were less frustrated or less angry at the conclusion of the interview than at its beginning?" (At this point, make a quick count of those people who have raised their hands to indicate reduced anger or frustration.) Then announce your count to the group.

- "How many of you who played the role of the employee were more angry or frustrated at the conclusion of the interview?" (At this point, make a quick count and announce it to the group.)

- "Those of you who were less angry or less frustrated, why was this the case?"

A variety of answers will now emerge. Responses should be placed on the chalkboard. They will probably include:

- Because request was granted.

- Supervisor will take it up with the next step in management, so there is a feeling something's being done.

- The supervisor listened.

- The supervisor showed concern.

- Now that the rule is understood, the loss of a day's pay is more acceptable.

- The supervisor appeared to be trying to figure out ways of dealing with the problem.

The instructor then asks:

> "*Those of you who were supervisors in the role play*, why do you think some employees were made angry or more frustrated at the end of the interview?"

Be sure to get answers from the *supervisors* themselves, not the employees. Answers from an employee could come as strong criticism against the person who conducted the interviewing. This should be avoided. Responses (which should be put on the chalkboard under the heading "Frustration Factors") to the questions which may emerge include:

- Because the request was not granted.

- Because the rules were enforced.

- Because the employee felt there was no concern for him or her (the employee).

- Because he or she felt he or she was not listened to.

- Because the supervisor was a difficult person.

The instructor then summarizes some of the key elements in the process part of the discussion. These points could include:

- Allow the person to fully express his or her view of the problem.

- Do not interrupt him or her.

- Attempt to listen carefully.

- Demonstrate that you fully understand his or her position by briefly summarizing to him or her (1) your perception of how he or she *feels* about the issue and (2) the *technical* basis of his or her complaint.

Superiors may be obliged to turn down a request after using this approach, but it is likely to reduce the employee's frustration or anger, even though he or she may not be totally satisfied with the outcome of the interview.

From the employee's point of view, the case is seen as an issue related to "fairness." Since the employee has been unaware of the new policy on days off for sick leave, he or she thinks it unfair to be docked one day's pay.

The supervisor, on the other hand, tends to think of the case in terms of a problem in making a decision of good quality. He or she usually gives first priority in making sure that the decision is consistent with management's overall personnel policies and procedures. Most supervisors also see that fairness is also an issue. To the extent that a supervisor would see these problems as "doing the correct managerial things," he or she probably will lean toward denying the employee's request. To the extent that he or she is more concerned with the fairness issue, he or she is more likely to take the case to the plant manager.

The instructor concludes with remarks along the following lines:

> In this section of the discussion, we have focused on the nature of interpersonal skills the supervisor uses in handling the employee's request. An important conclusion can now be drawn: A person who wants something from another person or organization can be satisfied in one of two ways (sometimes a combination):
>
> 1. *What he or she gets*: If a person gets a request granted for money, time off, or special considerations, this will probably satisfy him or her.
>
> 2. *How he or she is treated while making his or her request*: If a person is treated with fairness, concern, and understanding, he or she may accept a rejection of his or her request and still be happy.

In general, it is often easy to satisfy people for the moment by giving them those things they request. What is difficult is to handle situations where requests must be turned down or only partially met. In these situations, it is important for supervisors and managers to utilize their best knowledge and ability in interpersonal skills.

WALLACE WOHLKING is on the faculty of the New York State School of Industrial and Labor Relations, Cornell University. His articles on conflict resolution, attitude and behavior change, and management have appeared in *California Management Review, Training and Development Journal,* and *Personnel Journal.* He is co-author of a business game series titled *Handling Conflict in Management,* published by the American Management Association.

PATRICIA J. GILL is Director of Personnel for Bernard Hodes Advertising, Inc., active in the field of Recruitment Advertising and Employee Communications. Ms Gill was part of the team that developed FAIR PLAY, a training program presently on the market. She has also done work in the area of supervisory training utilizing behavior modeling, both as a consultant and as a training specialist at St. Luke's Hospital Center in Manhattan.